Addison-Wesley

ALGEBRA

Problem Bank

Created for use with *Addison-Wesley Algebra* Student Text

Stanley A. Smith
Randall I. Charles
John A. Dossey
Mervin L. Keedy
Marvin L. Bittinger

 Addison-Wesley Publishing Company

Menlo Park, California · Reading, Massachusetts · New York
Don Mills, Ontario · Wokingham, England
Amsterdam · Bonn · Sydney · Singapore · Tokyo
Madrid · San Juan

CONTRIBUTORS:

Michael Heaston, Ronan High School, Ronan, MT
Ernest Nielson, Glasgow High School, Glasgow, MT
Neil Tame, Oxford Hills School District, South Paris, ME
Dennis Wiser, Racine Unified School, Racine, WI

ISBN 0-201-25353-4

4 5 6 7 8 9 10 AL 9594939291

Contents

Strategy Problem Banks

A variety of problems are provided for each chapter that can be solved using nonroutine problem-solving techniques as well as the routine problem-solving techniques learned in *Addison-Wesley Algebra*. These problems are ideal for group-learning environments.

A suggested strategy for each problem is given with the answers. This is to be used as a hint, not a prescribed strategy. It is important for students to understand that there is more than one way to work a problem. The problem-solving experience can be enhanced by sharing a variety of methods.

See your teacher's edition of *Addison-Wesley Algebra* for suggested methods of teaching problem-solving ideas for group learning.

Solve using one or more strategies.

1. A bug is at the bottom of a glass jar that is 12 cm tall. The bug crawls up 2 cm every day and slides back 1 cm every night. How long will it take the bug to reach the top of the jar?

2. Carlos, Pat, Scott, Otis, Daniel, and Tom just finished a 1000-m race. Use the information below to determine the order in which they finished.
   Carlos finished 5 seconds behind Otis.
   Scott finished 2 seconds behind Otis and 15 seconds ahead of Pat.
   Pat beat Daniel by 10 seconds.
   Tom finished halfway between Carlos and Daniel.

3. Lian has sixteen coins worth $1.25. Some of her coins are dimes, and the rest are nickels. How many dimes does she have?

STRATEGY PROBLEM BANK 2
For use after Chapter 2

NAME _____

DATE _____

Solve using one or more strategies.

1. Maria, Josh, and Debra had a stack of posters to hang for the dance. They divided the posters evenly among themselves. After they had each hung six posters, the total number of posters left was the same as each person had to start with. How many posters did each student have to start with?

2. A survey of all the dogs and parakeets in a pet store shows that there are 15 heads and 42 feet. How many parakeets are there?

3. A 10 cm by 14 cm rectangular piece of cardboard has a 2 cm square cut out of each corner. Then the sides are folded up to form an open box. What is the volume of the box?

Solve using one or more strategies.

1. The pet store has a dog, a cat, a gerbil, a rabbit, and a parrot. If Ted buys two different pets, how many possible choices does he have?

2. A rectangle has a area of 110 cm². Its length and width are whole numbers. What are all the possibilities for the length and width? Which set of dimensions gives the greatest perimeter?

3. Lydia is going to make a long-distance call to her boyfriend from a pay phone. She has $2.60. If the phone company charges $0.80 for the first three minutes and $0.25 for each additional minute, for how many minutes can she talk?

Solve using one or more strategies.

1. Mrs. Brown, Mr. Green, and Mr. White live in houses that are brown, green, and white. None of these people has a house or a car of the same color as his or her last name. Mrs. Brown has a car that is the same color as Mr. White's house. What is the color of Mr. Green's house?

2. Stephanie placed trail markers along a 2000-m hiking trail. She placed one at the beginning, one at the end, and one marker every 200 m along the trail. How many markers did she use?

3. At Pinewood High School there are three academic clubs: Library Club, Science Club, and Mathematics Club. Five students are members of all three clubs. One third of the Library Club members and all of the Mathematics Club members belong to the Science Club. There are 24 members of the Library Club, 12 members of the Mathematics Club, and 39 members of the Science Club. How many students belong only to the Science Club?

Solve using one or more strategies.

1. Ms. Guzman assigned one problem the first day of school as homework. She assigned 5 problems the second day, 14 problems the third day, and 30 problems the fourth day. If she had continued this pattern, how many problems would she have assigned on the tenth day?

2. If there are 15 people in a room, and they each shake hands with every other person once, how many handshakes will there be?

3. In the small town of Jollyville (population 6561) jokes travel fast. In one hour each person who hears a joke tells three other people who have not heard the joke, and then tells no one else. One morning a salesperson from out of town told the barber a new joke. How long did it take for everyone in Jollyville to hear the joke?

Solve using one or more strategies.

1. In literature class you are asked to read three books from a reading list of six books. How many different sets of three books can you choose?

2. Inés opened a savings account at the bank. She deposited $75 the first week. The second week and each following week she deposited $8 more than she deposited the previous week. How much money has she put in her account after 7 weeks?

3. In a class election with five candidates, the winner beat the other four candidates by 3, 6, 7, and 11 votes, respectively. If 93 votes were cast, how many votes did the winner receive?

Solve using one or more strategies.

1. In art class the teacher asked each student to do a watercolor painting using two colors. If there are 18 different colors of watercolor paint available, then how many different color combinations are possible for the assignment?

2. What is the sum of the first 100 even, nonzero whole numbers? What is the sum of the first 100 odd whole numbers?

3. What is the ones' digit of the value of 2^{1005}?

Solve using one or more strategies.

1. The corner store sells pencils for $0.05, $0.10, and $0.15. How many different ways can Leon spend exactly $0.45 on pencils?

2. The Adventure Youth Hostel has men's and women's dorm rooms. The men's dorm rooms each have 13 beds. The women's dorm rooms each have 7 beds. If there are 134 beds in all, how many men's dorm rooms are there?

3. Colin was numbering the pages of his report. He started with 1 and typed 41 digits (using 0, 1, 2, 3, 4, 5, 6, 7, 8, and 9). How many pages does the report have?

NAME _____

DATE _____

Solve using one or more strategies.

1. Last year's pie eating champion planned to enter this year's pie eating contest. He went into training for 7 days. Each day he ate 2 more pies than he ate the day before. He ate a total of 112 pies while in training. How many pies did he eat the first day?

2. Dana loves canoeing. In 1 hour she travels 2 miles upstream using her strongest stroke. After working so hard, she has to rest for 30 minutes. During this time the canoe floats back downstream 1 mile. Continuing at the same rate of paddling and resting, how long would it take Dana to travel upstream 6 miles?

3. All gidgets are widgets. All widgets are hidgets. There are 24 gidgets. Eight hidgets are not widgets. There are 42 hidgets. How many widgets are not gidgets?

STRATEGY PROBLEM BANK 10
For use after Chapter 10

NAME _____

DATE _____

Solve using one or more strategies.

1. Colleen had some money. She gave $20 to her brother for his birthday, and spent $\frac{1}{2}$ of the remaining money for clothes. Then she bought gas for $15 and used $\frac{1}{5}$ of what was left for lunch. She saved the $20 that she had left. How much money did she have to start with?

2. In a sack of coins there are pennies, nickels, dimes, and quarters. There are twice as many quarters as nickels. There are 8 fewer dimes than quarters. There are 5 more nickels than pennies. There are 13 pennies. How many coins are there in the bag?

3. Four men were shipwrecked on an island. The first day they gathered a pile of coconuts and then went to sleep. During the night one of the men woke up and ate $\frac{1}{3}$ of the coconuts. A second man woke up and ate $\frac{1}{3}$ of the remaining coconuts. A third man did the same. When the fourth man woke up he ate $\frac{1}{4}$ of the remaining coconuts. Then there were 6 coconuts left. How many coconuts did the men gather?

Solve using one or more strategies.

1. A cube 3 cm × 3 cm × 3 cm is made up of 27 smaller cubes. The entire cube is painted red on the outside. How many of the 27 small cubes are painted red on 3 sides? How many are painted on 2 sides? How many are painted on 1 side? How many are painted on 0 sides?

2. A batting glove and a fielding glove together cost $44. The fielding glove costs 10 times as much as the batting glove. How much does each cost?

3. Kiri, Lon, Jane, and Dan each play a different sport: tennis, football, basketball, and water polo. Use the information below to determine which sport each plays.

   Jane doesn't own a tennis racquet.
   Kiri doesn't know how to swim.
   Neither Dan nor Jane were tall enough to make the basketball team.
   Lon plays football.

Solve using one or more strategies.

1. Toshi has 380 out of 440 points to date in algebra class. If there are 60 points remaining in the grading period, what is the least number of points she will need to have a grade of 80%? Grades are rounded to the nearest percent.

2. The sides of a hexagon are consecutive integers. If the perimeter is less than 40, what must be true about the length of the shortest side? What must be true about the length of the longest side?

3. You have two containers. One holds 4 cups and the other holds 9 cups. There are no markings on either container to indicate lesser quantities. How can you measure 6 cups of water using these two containers? There is an unlimited supply of water.

STRATEGY PROBLEM BANK 13
For use after Chapter 13

NAME _____

DATE _____

Solve using one or more strategies.

1. There are 14 teams in a basketball tournament. When a team loses a game they are eliminated from the tournament, and they play no more games. How many games are needed to determine the champion?

2. A bank offers either side-stub or top-stub checkbook covers. They have 7 color choices: red, blue, brown, tan, orange, black, or green. The customer may choose to have a name engraved on the checkbook cover or not. How many different choices are available for checkbook covers?

3. An engineer is trying to fill a water tank that is 25 m tall. Each day the pump runs, it raises the water level 3 m. There is a leak in the tank, and each night when the pump is turned off the water level drops 25 cm. At this rate, how many days will it take for the water to reach the top of the tank?

14   *Algebra Problem Bank*

© Addison-Wesley Publishing Company. All rights reserved.

Solve using one or more strategies.

1. Three consultants were hired by a company. The total consultant fees were $20,960. If Consultant 1 had made $700 less and Consultant 2 had made $200 more, each of the three would have been paid the same. How much did each consultant make?

2. Kea, Stacy, and Aaronica are the daughters of Mr. Chastain, Mr. DeMasi, and Mr. Bettis. Four of these people are playing badminton doubles. Mr. Bettis's daughter and Mr. Chastain are partners. Kea's father and Mr. DeMasi's daughter are also partners. There are no father-daughter combinations. Who is Kea's father?

3. Three years ago Luis invested some money at 10% interest. He now has $1000.01 in the account. If the interest was compounded yearly, how much money did he deposit 3 years ago?

NAME _____

DATE _____

Solve using one or more strategies.

1. Melissa scored 84, 78, 86, 91, and 70 on the five unit tests in algebra class. The 100-point final exam is worth 3 times as much as one unit test. What is the lowest grade Melissa can get on the final in order to average 85 for the course? Grades are rounded to the nearest whole number.

2. A farmer finds that from a herd of cattle, 60% of the calves born are male, and 95% of the male calves born survive the first year. What is the fewest number of calves that must be born for the farmer to have 100 male calves at the end of the first year?

3. $1^3 = 1$
   $1^3 + 2^3 = 9$
   $1^3 + 2^3 + 3^3 = 36$
   $1^3 + 2^3 + 3^3 + 4^3 = 100$
   $1^3 + 2^3 + 3^3 + 4^3 + 5^3 = 225$
   $1^3 + 2^3 + 3^3 + 4^3 + 5^3 + 6^3 = 441$

   What is the sum of the following?
   $1^3 + 2^3 + 3^3 + \ldots + 10^3$

Problem Banks

Additional problems are provided to accompany problem-solving lessons for supplementary practice with the specific techniques learned in each lesson.

Write as an algebraic expression.

1. Let a be Carol's age. Melissa is 5 years younger than Carol. Write an expression for Melissa's age.

   _____

2. Let p be the number of points scored by the Eagles. The Ramblers scored one third as many points as the Eagles. Write an expression for the Rambler's score.

   _____

3. Let c be the money Vito had before he was paid. Vito was paid $80. Write an expression for the amount of money Vito had after he was paid.

   _____

4. Let t be the amount that Ernest spent on T-shirts. Each of the six T-shirts that Ernest bought cost the same. Write an expression for the cost of one T-shirt.

   _____

5. Let a be the amount that Lynn earned last week. Lynn earned $23 less this week than she did last week. Write an expression for the amount that Lynn earned this week.

   _____

6. The perimeter of a rectangle is 24 and its width is x. Write an expression for its length.

   _____

7. Let s be Stephen's age 5 years from now. Write an expression for Stephen's age now.

   _____

8. Let j be Jewel's age 8 years ago. Write an expression for Jewel's age now.

   _____

9. The area of a rectangle is 72 mm^2 and its length is y. Write an expression for its width.

   _____

10. Let m be the number of magazines Stanley sold. Tomás sold 3 more than twice the number Stanley sold. Write an expression for the number of magazines Tomás sold.

    _____

PROBLEM BANK 2
For use with Lesson 2-3

Solve.

1. The PTA had a balance of $888.63 in their account at the beginning of the new school year. They donated $82.27 to the school for first-aid supplies. They deposited $295.00 from the sale of T-shirts and donated $70.00 for the principal to attend a conference. After these transactions, what was the new balance?

   _____

2. One morning in Barrow, Alaska, the temperature was −15°F. During the morning the temperature rose 12 degrees, but in the afternoon it dropped 8 degrees. What was the temperature after these changes had taken place?

   _____

3. After the kickoff of the football game, the Panthers passed for a short gain of 4 yards. They tried a quarterback sneak that resulted in a loss of 2 yards. Then they ran straight up the middle for a gain of 7 yards. How many yards were gained or lost in these three plays?

   _____

4. Lisa made $7.50 babysitting. She bought a new hair ribbon for $2.19, collected $5.00 that her sister owed her, paid $2.50 to go roller skating, and spent $1.25 playing video games. How much money did she have left?

   _____

5. The Small Town Water Company carefully monitors the water level in the main tank every two hours. The water level was 16 m at 8:00. By 10:00 the water level dropped 4 m, by noon it rose 3.5 m, by 2:00 it rose another 1.5 m, and by 4:00 the water level dropped 2.25 m. What was the water level at 4:00?

   _____

6. Big Bucks Investment Company recorded the following profits and losses over a 4-year period. Find the profit or loss for this period of time.

Year	Profit or loss
1985	− 12,500
1986	+ 3,467
1987	+ 31,783
1988	− 1,890

   _____

Solve.

1. A. W. Nardone had $423.78 in his checking account. He wrote a check for
   $657.89. What is the new balance in his checking account?

   _____

2. The temperature was 4°C at 9:00 p.m. By midnight the temperature had
   dropped to −3°C. How many degrees did the temperature fall?

   _____

3. There are 145 seniors in Forest Hills High School. If there is a total of 546
   students in the school, how many are not seniors?

   _____

4. Chen and Adrian went scuba diving. Chen went down to a depth of 123 ft.
   Adrian dove to a depth of 155 ft. How much deeper than Chen's dive was
   Adrian's?

   _____

5. Lorna parked her car 3 floors below ground-level in the lot of an office
   building. She got on the elevator and went up to the 19th floor. How many
   floors did the elevator go up?

   _____

6. A cold front moved into the area. The temperature went from 12°C to −2°C.
   If you were giving the local TV weather, how many degrees would you say
   the front changed the temperature?

   _____

7. In an exciting action-adventure movie, the pilot and copilot were thrown
   from a helicopter hovering 12 m above the surface of a lake. They plunged
   7 m below the water's surface before they were able to begin to swim to the
   surface. What was the length of their fall?

   _____

8. At the end of July, a small company had a balance of −$255 in its checkbook
   records. Nicole checked the records and found that a $298 deposit had not
   been recorded. What should the balance be for July?

   _____

9. Terry had $7.80 in the bank. The bank deducted a $12.00 service charge.
   What is Terry's new balance?

   _____

PROBLEM BANK 4
For use with Lesson 2-9

NAME _____

DATE _____

Write an equation that can be used to solve the problem.

1. Carl scored 16 points in the second basketball game. That was 4 more than he scored in the first game. How many points did he score in the first game?

   _____

2. There are 434 freshmen and sophomores in Lincoln High School. There are 215 sophomores. How many freshmen are there?

   _____

3. Ticket sales for the school play totaled $276.75. Tickets were $2.25 each. How many people purchased tickets?

   _____

4. A technician earned $154 for working seven hours. What is her hourly rate of pay?

   _____

5. A grocery store charges $2.55 for a six-ounce package of dried fruit and nuts. What is the cost of one ounce of the mix?

   _____

6. At the high school track meet, the score for the broad jump is the sum of each contestant's best two jumps. If Isaac's score was 5.4 m and his best jump was 3.1 m, what was his second best jump?

   _____

7. The boiling point of pure water is 100°C. This is 21.7°C higher than the boiling point of ethyl alcohol. What is the boiling point of ethyl alcohol?

   _____

8. A replica of the Statue of Liberty is $\frac{1}{5}$ the actual size of the statue. The replica is 18.5 m high. What is the height of the Statue of Liberty?

   _____

9. In a card game the total of all the scores must be 180 points. If one team makes 105 points, what is the score of the other team?

   _____

10. The area of a rectangle is 72 cm². The rectangle has a length of 9 cm. What is the width of the rectangle?

    _____

Translate to an equation and solve.

1. A number decreased by 12 is 17. What is the number?

_____

2. Forty more than Jan's age is 64. How old is Jan?

_____

3. If Sara paid $8750 for her new car, including $530 in options, what was the base price of the car (without options)?

_____

4. So Good green beans cost $0.86 per can. This is $0.32 more than Best Buy green beans. How much do Best Buy green beans cost?

_____

5. During the 1987 fund-raising project the Menlo High School Band sold 6864 calendars. This was 1259 more than they sold in 1986. How many calendars were sold during the 1986 fund-raising project?

_____

6. Jolon paid $130.98 for his new skateboard. This was $12.50 off the regular price. What was the regular price of the skateboard?

_____

7. At the end of the month the computer inventory indicated that there were 234 compact discs in stock. This was after sales of 347 and a restock of 56. How many compact discs were in stock at the beginning of the month?

_____

8. Lara's monthly salary is $234.78 more than Andy's salary. Lara's monthly salary is $1923.31. What is Andy's monthly salary?

_____

9. In Barrow, Alaska, the average daily low tempearture in January is $-37°C$. This is 49 degrees less than the average daily low temperature in Austin, Texas. What is the average daily low temperature in Austin in January?

_____

PROBLEM BANK 6

For use with Lesson 3-2

Translate to an equation and solve.

1. A number multiplied by 6 is -72. What is the number?

   _____

2. Two thirds of a number is 24. What is the number?

   _____

3. Harriet bought a bag of six maple bars for $1.14. What is the cost of one maple bar?

   _____

4. Sam sold his old car and bought a new one for $8750. The new car cost seven times as much as Sam got for his old car. How much money did he get for his old car?

   _____

5. A case of 2 dozen cans of soup costs $9.36. How much does a single can cost?

   _____

6. On Saturday, 129 people attended the basketball game. This was $\frac{1}{3}$ as many people as attended the basketball game last week. How many people went to the basketball game last week?

   _____

7. Cassette tape sales for last week were $1633.25. If each tape sold for $6.95, how many tapes were sold last week?

   _____

8. In 1986, Gadget Manufacturing Company made a profit of $678,900. This was only $\frac{2}{3}$ the profit that it earned in 1985. How much profit did the company make in 1985? How much did the profits decrease in 1986?

   _____

9. After attendance was taken, the school secretary recorded that 665 students were in school today. That is $\frac{19}{20}$ of the total number of students. How many students are there altogether?

   _____

10. Tommy has 1.2 times as much money saved as his sister. If Tommy has $84 saved, how much does his sister have saved?

   _____

Solve.

1. The formula for the volume of a cylinder is $V = \pi r^2 h$ where h is the height of the cylinder and r is the radius. Solve for r^2.

   _____

2. If an object is dropped, the formula for the distance it falls is $d = \frac{1}{2}gt^2$ where t is the time in seconds and g is the acceleration due to gravity. Solve for g.

   _____

3. If an object is thrown, the formula for the distance it travels is $s = vt + \frac{1}{2}gt^2$ where v is the initial speed of the object, t is the time in seconds, and g is the acceleration due to gravity. Solve for v.

   _____

4. Solve the formula for the distance a thrown object travels (given in Problem 3) for g.

   _____

5. The amount a that a principal p will be worth after t years at interest rate r, compounded annually, is given by the formula $a = p(1 + r)^t$. Solve for p.

   _____

6. The formula for the circumference of a circle is $c = 2\pi r$ where r is the radius of the circle. Solve for π.

   _____

7. The formula for the perimeter of a rectangle is $P = 2l + 2w$. Solve for w.

   _____

8. The formula $F = 1.8C + 32$ can be used to convert from Celsius temperature (C) to Fahrenheit temperature (F). Solve for C.

   _____

9. The distance that an object travels can be expressed by the formula $s = 4.9t^2 + vt$, where t is the time in seconds and v is the initial speed of the object. Solve for v.

   _____

10. Any line can be expressed by the formula $y - y_1 = m(x - x_1)$ where (x_1, y_1) is a point on the line and m is the slope of the line. Solve for m.

    _____

PROBLEM BANK 8
For use with Lesson 3-9

NAME _____

DATE _____

Write a proportion and solve.

1. If three out of every seven students are going on a field trip, how many will be going if there are 854 students in the school?

   _____

2. The ratio of chickens to ducks in the barnyard is 7 to 5. If there are 91 chickens, how many ducks are there?

   _____

3. In an enormous jar of marbles, the ratio of red to green marbles is 13 to 5. If there are 600 green marbles, how many red marbles are in the jar?

   _____

4. A glass company estimates that it takes 15 minutes to install 2 windows. In a large construction project there are 124 windows to be installed. How many hours will it take to install these windows?

   _____

5. A car travels 47 miles on 2 gallons of gasoline. How many miles can it travel on 17 gallons of gasoline?

   _____

6. On a map 1 cm represents 25 km. There are 3.8 cm between two cities on the map. What is the actual distance between the two cities?

   _____

7. In a recent political poll, 500 people were surveyed. The responses showed that 232 people favored candidate Kahn over candidate Waller. If this survey is representative of the 52,000 voters in the district, how many voters favor candidate Kahn?

   _____

8. In a lake, the ratio of trout to carp is 7 to 11. If there is a total of 756 fish, how many are carp?

   _____

9. In a recent basketball game the Reds outscored the Spartans at a ratio of 5 to 2. If a total of 98 points were scored, how many points were scored by the Spartans?

   _____

Solve.

1. On a test of 60 items, Ray got 45 correct. What percent of the items were correct?

   _____

2. A salesperson's quota is $2250 for one month. Last month the salesperson sold merchandise totaling $2587.50. What percent of the quota did the salesperson meet?

   _____

3. The Woods have a house payment of $627.90 per month. This is 23% of their monthly income. What is their monthly income?

   _____

4. The sales tax rate in Birmingham, Alabama, is 7%. How much tax must Claire pay if she buys a television for $346.20? How much is the total cost of her purchase?

   _____

5. The volume of ice decreases 8.3% when it is thawed. If 550 cm³ of ice are thawed, how much will the volume of the ice decrease? What will be the volume of the water?

   _____

6. Sales tax in Quitman is 4%. What would the sales tax be on a scooter costing $140? What is the total cost of the scooter, including sales tax?

   _____

7. A catalog store promises 10% off everything in its catalog except compact disc players, which will be only 5% off. Ted paid $264 for a stereo amplifier and a compact disc player that he ordered from the catalog. The list price (before discount) of the stereo amplifier was $135. What was the list price (before discount) of the compact disc player?

   _____

8. The population of grizzly bears in Montana is growing at the rate of 2% each year. It is estimated that there are now 4500 grizzly bears in Montana. At this rate, how many bears should there be one year from now? How many bears should there be two years from now?

   _____

Solve.

1. Forty more than twice Malia's age is 64. Find Malia's age.

   _____

2. Find three consecutive integers whose sum is 90.

   _____

3. Find three consecutive even integers whose sum is 84.

   _____

4. A camera sells for $100. This is $10 less than twice the price of the camera last year. What was the price of the camera last year?

   _____

5. The second side of a triangle is 3 in. longer than the first side. The third side is twice as long as the first side. If the perimeter of the triangle is 23 in., how long is each side?

   _____

6. After a 15% discount, an item was sold for $61.20. What was the original price of the item?

   _____

7. Toshio put some money into a savings account and deposited no more into this account for one year. At the end of the year, there was $5885 in the account, including 7% of the original amount for interest. How much did he deposit originally?

   _____

8. The number of students in Central High School was 1225 in 1986. The number of students enrolled in 1987 was 4% less than in 1986. How many students were enrolled in 1987?

   _____

9. An overnight delivery company charges $12.54 for the first 12 oz and $0.72 per ounce for each ounce over 12 oz. If it costs $17.58 to send a package, what does it weigh?

   _____

10. The Lions have won 40 of their first 74 baseball games. How many of the remaining 66 games must the team win to win 60% of their games?

    _____

Solve.

1. The sum of three consecutive even integers is less than 75. What are the greatest possible values of these integers?

   _____

2. Find the greatest possible pair of integers such that one integer is 3 more than twice the other and their sum is less than 42.

   _____

3. The sum of two integers is greater than 23. One integer is 5 less than 3 times the other. What are the least values of the integers?

   _____

4. The length of a rectangle is 5 cm more than twice the width, and the perimeter is greater than 28 cm. What is the width of the rectangle?

   _____

5. Jim is selling greeting cards at a booth at a folk fair. He will be paid $12 plus $2 for each box that he sells. How many boxes must he sell in order to make at least $42?

   _____

6. Gail works for a vending company. She gets paid $64 per week plus 20% of her total sales. How much will her total sales for the week have to be in order for Gail to make at least $200?

   _____

7. Ms. Norman's company gave her $285 for hotel and meals for a three-day business trip. Ms. Norman plans to spend $52 per night on a hotel room. What is the most she can spend per day on meals and stay within this travel budget?

   _____

8. How long must the sides of an equilateral triangle be in order for the perimeter to be greater than 45 m?

   _____

9. The base of a triangle is 8 cm. What height will make the area greater than 32 cm²?

   _____

PROBLEM BANK 12
For use with Lesson 6-9

NAME _____

DATE _____

Translate to an equation and solve.

1. The product of two consecutive positive even integers is 48. Find the two integers.

   _____

2. One side of a rectangle is 4 in. longer than the other. If the sides are each increased by 2 in., the area of the new rectangle is 60 in². How long are the sides of the original rectangle?

   _____

3. The sum of the squares of two consecutive even integers is 244. Find the two integers.

   _____

4. The sum of twice a number and the number squared is −1. What is this number?

   _____

5. Five times a number decreased by 6 is equal to the number squared. What is the number?

   _____

6. An object is dropped from the top of a tower. The formula $s = 4.9t^2$ gives the distance in meters (s) that the object falls in t seconds. How many seconds will it take the object to fall 122.5 m?

   _____

7. Mr. Ford has a square garden in his backyard. He increased the length of each side by 2 m. After he enlarged the garden it had an area of 196 m². What was the measure of the sides of the garden before it was enlarged? How much did the change in the length of the sides increase the area of the garden?

   _____

8. The cube of a number is the same as 3 times its square. Find the number.

   _____

9. The length of a rectangle is twice the width. If the length is decreased by 1 and the width increased by 3, the area is 72 mm². Find the original length and width.

   _____

PROBLEM BANK 13
For use with Lesson 7-7

Solve. Assume a linear relationship fits each set of data.

1. An overnight delivery company advertised the following rates: a 6-oz (w) package for $6.98 ($c$) and a 12-oz ($w$) package for $8.18 ($c$). Use the data points ($w$, c).
   a. Find a linear equation for these data points.
   b. Use this linear equation to find the cost of sending a 32-oz package.

   _____

2. A temperature of 0°C is the same as a temperature of 273.15 K. A temperature of 100°C is the same as a temperature of 373.15 K. Use the ordered pairs (C, K).
   a. Find a linear equation for these data points.
   b. Use this linear equation to find the Kelvin temperature when the temperature is 30°C.

   _____

3. A temperature of 32°F is the same as a temperature of 273.15 K. A temperature of 80.33°F is the same as a temperature of 300 K. Use the data points (K, F).
   a. Find a linear equation for these data points.
   b. Use this linear equation to find the temperature Fahrenheit when the temperature is 373.15°K.

   _____

4. Height and ideal weight are related linearly. An adult person who is 150 cm (h) tall has an ideal weight of 50 kg (w). A person who is 200 cm tall has an ideal weight of 90 kg. Use the data points (h, w).
   a. Find a linear equation for these data points.
   b. Use this linear equation to find the ideal weight of a person who is 165 cm tall.

   _____

5. Taxi fare for a 5-km (d) trip is $3.75 ($f$). The fare for a 10-km trip is $6.75. Use the data points (d, f).
   a. Find a linear equation for these data points.
   b. Use this linear equation to find the taxi fare for a 32-km trip.

   _____

6. In an exercise program, the recommended maximum heartbeat rate during exercise is 168 beats per minute (b) for a 10-year-old (a). The recommended maximum heartbeat rate during exercise for a 40-year-old is 144 beats per minute. Use the data points (a, b).
   a. Find a linear equation for these data points.
   b. Use this linear equation to find the recommended maximum heartbeat rate for exercise for a 15-year-old.

   _____

Translate to a system of equations and solve.

1. The sum of two numbers is 39. One number is 7 more than the other. Find the two numbers.

   _____

2. The difference between two numnbers is 12. The larger number is three times the smaller. What are the numbers?

   _____

3. Find two numbers whose sum is 41 and whose difference is 17.

   _____

4. Find two numbers whose difference is 22 and the larger is 2 more than twice the smaller.

   _____

5. The difference between two numbers is 9. Three times the smaller is equal to twice the larger. What are the numbers?

   _____

6. The sum of two numbers is 14. The sum of twice the first and three times the second is 34. Find the numbers.

   _____

7. The sum of two numbers is -4 and their difference is -10. Find the numbers.

   _____

8. The difference between two numbers is 23. The larger is 29 more than twice the smaller. What are the numbers?

   _____

9. The first number is 5 less than the second number. Four times the first number plus 5 times the second number is 74. Find the numbers.

   _____

10. The perimeter of a rectangle is 58 cm. The length is 7 cm less than three times the width. Find the length and width.

    _____

Translate to a system of equations and solve.

1. The sum of two numbers is 63. One ninth of the first number plus one sixth of the second number is 21. Find the numbers.

   _____

2. The difference between two numbers is 35. One half the larger number plus one third the smaller is 30. Find the numbers.

   _____

3. The sum of two numbers is 97. Their difference is 31. What are the numbers?

   _____

4. The sum of two numbers is 23.6. One is four times the other. Find the numbers.

   _____

5. The sum of twice the first number and three times the second is 10. The sum of one seventh the first number and two thirds the second number is −2. What are the numbers?

   _____

6. The sum of twice the first number and eight times the second is 7. Six times the first is equal to four times the second. Find the numbers.

   _____

7. Two angles are complementary. One is 6° more than three times the other. Find the angles. (Complementary angles have a sum of 90°.)

   _____

8. Two angles are supplementary. One is 60° more than one half the other. Find the angles. (Supplementary angles have a sum of 180°.)

   _____

9. The perimeter of a rectangle is 332 cm. The length is 7 cm more than twice the width. Find the length and width of the rectangle.

   _____

10. The sum of twice the first number and three times the second is −10. Five times the first less twice the second is 51. What are the numbers?

    _____

PROBLEM BANK 16
For use with Lesson 8-4

Translate to a system of equations and solve.

1. In 5 years Chim will be three times as old as Jared. The sum of their ages is 42. How old are Chim and Jared?

2. Case High School sold 120 tickets to the school play and took in $195 from ticket sales. If student tickets were $1 and adult tickets were $2, how many of each kind did they sell?

3. A group of students went hiking in a wildlife sanctuary. During the hike a total of 180 ticks and mosquitoes were slapped. If these pests had a total of 1240 legs, how many mosquitoes and how many ticks were slapped during the hike? (Hint: Ticks have 8 legs and mosquitoes have 6 legs.)

4. In a library there are rectangular tables having four legs and hexagonal tables having six legs. Plastic caps must be placed on the legs to protect the floor. The job will take 112 caps, and there are 13 more rectangular tables than hexagonal ones. How many of each kind of table are there in the library?

5. There are 22 student taking the late bus home. There are 14 more girls than boys on the bus. How many girls and how many boys are taking the late bus?

6. The sum of Elisa's age and Ira's age is 47. Ira's age is 5 years less than three times Elisa's age. How old are Ira and Elisa?

7. Gil has $2 more than Karen. Together they have $70. How much money does each person have?

8. Barbara bought a pair of dress shoes and a pair of sport shoes. The combined cost was $90.48. The dress shoes cost $15.88 less than the sport shoes. Find the cost of each pair of shoes.

9. A sweatshirt with a name costs $8.95, and a sweatshirt with a picture of a rock band costs $9.50. If 30 sweatshirts were sold one day for a total of $272.90, how many of each kind were sold?

Solve.

1. Betty leaves her purse in a store at the mall and averages 36 mi/h on her way home to Glenville, 140 miles away. Honest Harry discovers her purse and starts after her one hour later. If he averages 48 mi/h, how long will it take him to catch Betty? Will he catch her before she reaches Glenville?

   _____

2. Fred leaves the corner of Maple Avenue and Front Street on his bicycle, and travels west at 14 km/h. Two hours later Celia leaves the same corner and walks east at 5 km/h. How many hours does it take for Fred and Celia to be 104 km apart?

   _____

3. A small plane left Chicago at 11:00 p.m. and traveled at 180 mi/h. A jet left Chicago and traveled in the same direction at 720 mi/h. If the jet left Chicago at 2:00 a.m., at what time will the jet overtake the small plane?

   _____

4. A thief flees San Francisco and heads toward Los Angeles driving at a rate of 80 km/h. Five minutes after the thief leaves, a deputy sheriff begins chasing the thief and drives at 100 km/h. How long will it be before the deputy sheriff catches up with the thief?

   _____

5. Julie and George can row at the same rate in still water. They leave Carston at the same time, Julie going upstream and George going downstream. Julie rows for two hours and arrives in Polton, 3 miles from Carston. George rows for three hours and arrives at Burnburg, 13.5 miles from Carston. Find the rate of the current and the rate each rows in still water.

   _____

6. Dr. White leaves home to drive to a convention. She is traveling at 55 mi/h. She is 10 mi from home when her husband realizes she has forgotten her briefcase. How fast will he have to drive to catch her in two hours?

   _____

7. It is 280 miles from Memphis to Birmingham. An express train left Memphis traveling toward Birmingham at 70 mi/h. Two hours earlier a freight train left Birmingham traveling toward Memphis on a parallel track. The speed of this train was 50 mi/h. How long was it before the two trains met?

   _____

Translate to a system of equations and solve.

1. Adriana has 24 dimes and nickels in a jar. The total value of the coins in the jar is $2.10. How many of each coin does she have?

   _____

2. The sum of the digits of a two-digit number is 16. If the digits are reversed, the original number minus the new number is 18. Find the original number.

   _____

3. A farmer sold bushels of wheat and bushels of oats. For 425 bushels, he received $481.58. How many bushels of each did he sell, if he received $2.08 per bushel of wheat and $0.94 per bushel of oats?

   _____

4. Gretchen has $8.75 in dimes and quarters in her purse. If she has 65 coins, how many quarters are in her purse?

   _____

5. The units' digit of a two-digit number is 5 less than twice the tens' digit. If the digits are reversed, the new number is 9 less than the original number. Find the number.

   _____

6. Mr. Smythe took two of his children to the theater and the cost of the tickets was $8.50. The next week Mr. Smythe, Mrs. Smythe, and all five children went back to the theater, and the cost of the tickets was $19.25. How much would it cost if Mr. Smythe and Mrs. Smythe went alone?

   _____

7. On the first day of a new job, Mike was sent to a bakery by his boss. Each of 18 workers gave him an order for either a roll or a bran muffin. The rolls cost $0.40 each, and the muffins cost $0.55 each. His boss wrote a company check for $9.15. On the way to the store Mike lost the order, but was able to figure out what the order had to be. What was the order?

   _____

8. Mr. Griffith rolls the coins from his vending machines to take them to the bank. After rolling coins one evening he had 38 coins left over, totaling $2.45. All of these coins were nickels and dimes. How many were nickels and how many were dimes?

   _____

Solve.

1. Everett can type a 60-page paper in 8 hours. Laverne can type a 60-page paper in 12 hours. How long will it take them to type 60 pages if they work together?

   _____

2. Helen can paint a living room in 5 hours. If Bill helps Helen they can paint the room in 3 hours. How long would it take Bill to paint the living room alone?

   _____

3. The reciprocal of 3 plus the reciprocal of 7 is the reciprocal of what number?

   _____

4. Virginia can deliver the papers on her paper route in 30 minutes. When her brother Wayne takes the route, it takes him 40 minutes. How long does it take if they deliver the papers together?

   _____

5. Dennis paints three times as fast as Juanita. Working together, they can paint a house in 12 hours. How long would it take either of them working alone?

   _____

6. One pump can fill a tank in 8 hours. The backup pump can fill the tank in 10 hours. If both pumps are used, how long will it take to fill the tank?

   _____

7. The sum of one third of a number and its reciprocal is the same as 49 divided by the number. Find the number.

   _____

8. The additive inverse of a number divided by 16 is the same as 1 less than -5 times its reciprocal. Find the number.

   _____

9. The button factory just bought a new button press. The new press is three times faster than the old press. Operating together they can produce a gross of buttons in 12 minutes. How long would it take each press to produce a gross of buttons separately?

   _____

Solve.

1. Solution A is 30% acid and solution B is 70% acid. How much of each should be used to make 100 mL of a solution that is 58% acid?

   _____

2. Solution A is 20% alcohol and solution B is 60% alcohol. How much of each should be used to make 100 L of a solution that is 45% alcohol?

   _____

3. A dairy has 50 gallons of milk that is 7.8% butterfat. How much skim milk (no butterfat) should be mixed with it to make milk that is 2% butterfat?

   _____

4. A vat contains 400 L of a solution that is 32% acid. How much water should be added to make a solution that is 25% acid?

   _____

5. A chemist has 25% chloride solution and 70% chloride solution. She needs 75 oz of 50% chloride solution. How much of the 25% and 70% solutions can be mixed to produce the desired quantity of 50% chloride solution?

   _____

6. The Peanut Pub has pecans that sell for $7.50 per kilogram and almonds that sell for $8.75 per kilogram. The owner wants to make a 10-kg mixture of these two varieties, which will sell for $8.00 per kilogram. How many kilograms of each variety will he need to use to produce the desired mixture?

   _____

7. Robin's company invested its profits of $52,700, part at 13.5% and part at 15%. The total annual yield on this investment was $7432.50. How much was invested at each rate?

   _____

8. Alice's grandfather uses brine solution to make pickles. He has 8 gallons of 5% brine solution (5% salt and 95% water). How much of this solution should be poured out and replaced with water to result in a 3% brine solution?

   _____

9. A chainsaw runs on fuel that is 10% oil and 90% gas. How much oil will have to be added to 3 gallons of fuel that is 5% oil and 95% gas in order to use it in the chainsaw?

   _____

Solve. Round answers to the nearest tenth.

1. A castle is protected by a 20-ft moat and walls whose lowest points are 32 ft above the ground. Attackers have built ladders that are 35 ft long. Will they be able to get over the wall? Explain.

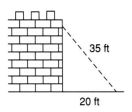

35 ft

20 ft

_____

2. The gate shown is made with wood 6 in. wide. Is a board 5 ft 10 in. long enough to make the cross brace?

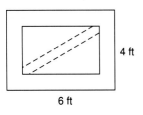

4 ft

6 ft

_____

3. All the roads in the sketch below are in need of repair. The Polson-Pablo road and the Ronan-Pablo road will cost $22,000 per mile to repair, but the Ronan-Polson road, because it runs through a swamp, will cost $26,000 per mile to repair. Would it be less costly to repair the road running through the swamp or the roads around the swamp from Polson to Ronan? By how much?

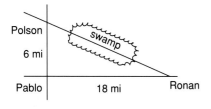

Polson

6 mi

Pablo   18 mi   Ronan

_____

4. The diagonal of a square measures 12 cm. How long are the sides of the square?

_____

5. The legs of an isosceles right triangle each measure 7 in. How long is the third side?

_____

Solve.

The formula $V = 3.5\sqrt{h}$ tells how many kilometers (V) you can see from a height of h meters above sea level. Use this formula for problems 1-3. Approximate answers to the nearest whole number.

1. How far can you see to the horizon from the highest point in Arkansas, Magazine Mountain, which has an elevation of 839 m?

_____

2. From the top of Cheaha Mountain in Alabama you can see about 95 km. How high is Cheaha Mountain?

_____

3. From the top of the highest mountain in California, Mount Whitney, you can see about 233 km. How high is Mount Whitney?

_____

The formula $r = 2\sqrt{5L}$ can be used to approximate the speed (r), in mi/h, of a car that has left a skid mark of length L, in feet. Use this formula in problems 4 and 5.

4. How far will a car skid at 30 mi/h?

_____

5. How far will a car skid at 80 mi/h?

_____

6. Find a number such that three times its square root is 24.

_____

7. Find a number such that the square root of 3 less than 7 times the number is 5.

_____

8. Find a number such that the additive inverse of twice its square root is −18.

_____

9. The formula $t = \sqrt{\dfrac{2s}{g}}$ gives the time in seconds for an object, initially at rest, to fall s feet. If $g = 32.2$, find the distance an object falls in the first 3 seconds.

_____

NAME _____

DATE _____

Write a linear function describing each situation. Use the function to solve the problem.

1. Ella works at a plant store. She is paid $24.00 per day plus $1.25 for every plant she sells. How much will she earn if she sells 23 plants today?

_____

2. More Sports Athletic Store charges $35 to set up a silk-screen pattern for printing T-shirts for soccer teams, and $6.75 for each T-shirt. If the Big Town Soccer League orders 180 T-shirts, how much will the total cost be?

_____

3. A 50-cm spring will stretch (in cm) one fourth the weight (in kg) attached to it. How long will the spring be if a 16-kg weight is attached?

_____

4. The Rent-an-Oldie Car-Rental Company charges $15 per day plus $0.12 per mile. Find the cost of a one-day trip of 240 miles.

_____

5. The Phone Home Long-Distance Company charges $0.50 per long-distance call plus $0.20 per minute. What would it charge for a ten-minute call?

_____

6. The cost of renting a carpet shampooer is $12.75 per day plus $9.98 for the shampoo. What would it cost to rent the shampooer for two days?

_____

7. A car-rental company is having a special. You can rent a car for $45 per day with unlimited mileage. Collision insurance costs $8.75. How much would it cost to rent a car for 5 days if you buy the insurance?

_____

8. A water company has a base charge of $5.15. The charge for the water you use is $4.80 per thousand gallons. If you use 1500 gallons of water, how much is the bill?

_____

9. Mr. Fixit Repair Service charges $30 for a service call, plus $15 per hour after the first hour. If a repair call takes one hour and forty-five minutes, what is the charge?

_____

PROBLEM BANK 24
For use with Lesson 12-5

NAME _____

DATE _____

Find and use an equation of variation to solve.

1. The price (p) of a choice steak varies directly as its weight (w). For a steak weighing 6.5 oz the price is $2.86. Find the cost of a steak weighing 8 oz.

    _____

2. The weight (E) of an object on Earth varies directly as its weight (M) on the moon. An object that weighs 38 lb on the moon will weigh 230 lb on Earth. How much would an object weighing 57 lb on the moon weigh on Earth?

    _____

3. The distance between two cities is 275 miles. They are shown 5.5 cm apart on a map. How far apart are two cities that are shown 8 cm apart on the same map?

    _____

4. The Social Security deduction on your paycheck varies directly with your earnings. If your earnings are $2000, then the Social Security deduction is $143. What will the Social Security deduction be if you earn $3500?

    _____

5. At a large company the employees' hourly wage increases vary directly with the job rating. An employee with a job rating of 2 receives a salary increase of $0.12 per hour. What will your salary increase be if your job rating is 5?

    _____

6. The perimeter of a regular hexagon varies directly as the length of the sides. A regular hexagon with perimeter 42 m has sides of length 7 m. What is the perimeter of a regular hexagon with sides 3.5 m?

    _____

7. The cost of building a new house varies directly with the number of square feet in the house. A house with 1500 ft^2 costs $81,000. What would be the cost of a house containing 1200 ft^2?

    _____

8. At Johnston's Grocery Store the retail price of an item varies directly as the wholesale price. For an item with a retail cost of $0.96 the wholesale cost is $0.80. What is the retail cost of an item that costs $2.10 wholesale?

    _____

Find and use an equation of variation to solve.

1. If it costs $19.60 per person for 5 people to charter a party barge, what will it cost per person for 8 people to charter the barge?

    _____

2. The number of revolutions of a tire rolling over a given distance varies inversely as the circumference of the tire. If a tire with a circumference of 70 in. turns 3 revolutions to cover a set distance, then how many revolutions will a tire with a circumference of 30 in. have to turn to cover the same distance? What is the distance?

    _____

3. The length of rectangles of fixed area varies inversely as the width. Suppose the length of a rectangle is 22 mm when the width is 12 mm. Find the width when the length is 33 mm. What is the fixed area?

    _____

4. The time required to fill a tank varies inversely as the rate of pumping. A pump can fill a tank in 45 minutes at the rate of 1350 L/min. How long will it take the pump to fill the tank at 900 L/min? How many liters does the tank hold?

    _____

5. The time it takes to make a trip varies inversely as the speed of travel. If it takes 3 hours and 15 minutes to make the trip at 60 mi/h, how long will it take to make the trip at 50 mi/h? How far is the trip?

    _____

6. The current in an electrical conductor varies inversely as the resistance of the conductor. The current is 4 amperes when the resistance is 480 ohms. What is the current when the resistance is 384 ohms?

    _____

7. The time it takes a runner to complete a race varies inversely as his running speed. If a runner runs at a speed of 200 m per minute it will take him 50 minutes to complete the race. If a runner runs at 500 m per minute, how long will it take him to complete the race? How long is the race?

    _____

8. The height of rectangular prisms of fixed volume varies inversely as the area of the base. Suppose the area of the base is 30 cm^2 when the height is 6 cm. Find the height when the area of the base is 18 cm^2. What is the fixed volume?

    _____

PROBLEM BANK 26
For use with Lesson 13-7

NAME _____

DATE _____

Solve.

1. A picture frame is 22 cm by 10 cm. There are 160 cm² of picture showing. Find the width of the frame.

   _____

2. The hypotenuse of a right triangle is 13 m. One leg is 7 m longer than the other leg. Find the lengths of the legs.

   _____

3. The length of a rectangle is 3 cm less than twice its width. Its area is 170 cm². Find the length and width of the rectangle.

   _____

4. The current in a stream is 4 km/h. A boat travels 24 km upstream and 24 km downstream in a total time of 8 hours. What is the speed of the boat in still water?

   _____

5. Walkways are placed along one side and one end of a rectangular garden. The width of the walk along the end is twice the width of the walk along the side. The length of the garden (including walks) is 20 m, the width 15 m. The area of the garden reserved for planting is 208 m². Find the width of the walkways.

   _____

6. A circular picture frame has a diameter of 10 cm. There are 20.25π cm² of picture showing. What is the width of the frame?

   _____

7. Stanley and Kathleen were making a car trip together. Stanley drove 10 mi/h faster than Kathleen. Stanley drove 120 miles and Kathleen drove 150 miles in a total of 5 hours. How fast did each of them drive?

   _____

8. The diagonal of a rectangle is 1 in. longer than the length of the rectangle, and the rectangle's length is 1 in. longer than its width. Find the length and width of the rectangle and the measure of the diagonal.

   _____

9. The base of a triangle is 5 mm more than its height. The area of the triangle is 7 mm². Find the base and height.

   _____

Solve. Round to the nearest tenth.

1. A guy wire runs from the ground to the top of a telephone pole. The angle of elevation is 34°, and the guy wire is 11 m long. How tall is the telephone pole?

   _____

2. A kite is flown with 52 m of string. The angle of elevation is 48°. How high is the kite?

   _____

3. A tower is 48 m tall. The angle of depression from the top of the tower to an anchor point on the ground is 16°. How long an anchor wire is needed to run from the top of the tower to the anchor point?

   _____

4. A building is 140 m from a radio tower. From the top of the building the angle of elevation and the angle of depression to the top and bottom of the tower is 65° and 13°, respectively. Find the height of the tower.

   _____

5. A man is standing 6 ft from a wall. The angle of depression from the top of his head to the bottom of the wall is 47°. The angle of elevation from the top of his head to the top of the wall is 38°. How tall is the man? How tall is the wall?

   _____

6. The firing angle of a missile was 22°. It has traveled 234 m along the firing line. How far away from the firing site is the ground point below the missile?

   _____

7. A rocket is launched at an angle of 36°. About how high is it after it has traveled 530 m?

   _____

8. The angle of elevation of a bird is 14°. The distance to the bird is 3 km. How high is the bird?

   _____

9. You have climbed 20 m up an observation tower. You estimate the angle of depression to your car is 40°. How far is your car from the foot of the tower?

   _____

10. Mary is walking toward her office building, which she knows is 150 ft tall. The angle to the top of the building from where she is standing is 6°. How far does she have to walk?

   _____

College Entrance Exams

This section contains four exams that simulate the PSAT exams, which are given for college entrance. An answer sheet containing sets of answer blanks identical to those used for PSAT exams is provided to familiarize students with the PSAT answer format.

Exam 1

Time—50 minutes
50 Questions

In this section solve each problem, using any available space on the page for scratchwork. Then decide which is the best of the choices given and blacken the corresponding oval on the answer sheet.

The following information is for your reference in solving some of the problems.

Circle of radius r:
Area $= \pi r^2$
Circumference $= 2\pi r$
The number of degrees of arc in a circle is 360.

The measure in degrees of a straight angle is 180.

Triangle:
The sum of the measures in degrees of the angles of a triangle is 180.

If $\angle CDA$ is a right angle, then

(1) area of $\triangle ABC = \dfrac{AB \times CD}{2}$

(2) $AC^2 = AD^2 + DC^2$

Definitions of symbols:
$=$ is equal to
$\neq$ is unequal to
$<$ is less than
$>$ is greater than
$\leq$ is less than or equal to
$\geq$ is greater than or equal to
$\parallel$ is parallel to
$\perp$ is perpendicular to

Note: Figures that accompany problems in this test are intended to provide information useful in solving the problems. They are drawn as accurately as possible EXCEPT when it is stated in a specific problem that its figure is not drawn to scale. All figures lie in a plane unless otherwise indicated. All numbers used are real numbers.

1. If $x - 3 = 15 - x$, then $x =$
   (A) 6   (B) -6 (C) 9   (D) 18   (E) -9

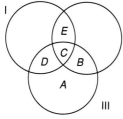

2. In the figure above, which lettered region is common to circles I and II, but not part of III?
   (A) A (B) B (C) C (D) D (E) E

---

3. How many 10¢ pencils can be purchased for D dollars?
   (A) $\dfrac{D}{100}$ (B) $\dfrac{D}{10}$ (C) D (D) $10D$
   (E) $100D$

---

4. What is the greatest integer that is a factor of 840, 1200, and 1400?
   (A) 7   (B) 8   (C) 15   (D) 30   (E) 40

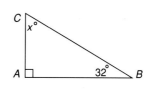

5. In $\triangle ABC$ above, what is the value of x?
   (A) 32   (B) 58   (C) 68   (D) 90   (E) 12

---

6. How much can be saved by buying a stereo for $185 in cash rather than paying $20 down and six monthly payments of $31 each?
   (A) $11   (B) $15   (C) $20   (D) $21
   (E) $26

---

7. $-(-2)(-3)(-4)(-5)$ is equal to which of the following expressions?
   (A) $-2 - 3 - 4 - 5$

   (B) $-[-2 - 3 - 4 - 5]$

   (C) $[2 - (3 + 4 + 5)]$

   (D) $2 \cdot 3 \cdot 4 \cdot 5$

   (E) $2(-3)(-4)(-5)$

---

8. If $\left(p + \dfrac{1}{2}\right) + \left(p - \dfrac{1}{2}\right) = 3$, then $p =$
   (A) $\dfrac{2}{3}$ (B) $\dfrac{3}{2}$ (C) $\dfrac{5}{2}$ (D) 3   (E) $\dfrac{7}{2}$

---

9. 36 is $\dfrac{3}{8}$ of what number?

   (A) 96   (B) 16   (C) 72   (D) 80   (E) $13\dfrac{1}{2}$

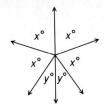

10. In the figure above, if $x = 2y$, then $y =$
    (A) 36 (B) 72 (C) 60 (D) 30 (E) 70

Questions 11–12 refer to the following definition.

For all m, n, r, and t such that $mr \neq nt$,

$$\frac{m \mid n}{r \mid t} = \frac{mn - rt}{mr - nt}.$$

11. $\dfrac{3 \mid -2}{-3 \mid 2} =$

    (A) $-\dfrac{12}{5}$ (B) $-\dfrac{1}{5}$ (C) 0 (D) $\dfrac{1}{5}$ (E) $\dfrac{12}{5}$

---

12. $\dfrac{\dfrac{1 \mid 1}{1 \mid 2} \, 1}{1 \quad 2} =$

    (A) -2

    (B) -1

    (C) 0

    (D) 1

    (E) 2

---

13. A line segment has endpoints $(-3, 5)$ and $(1, 7)$. What are the coordinates of the midpoint?

    (A) $(-2, 12)$ (B) $(-4, -2)$ (C) $(-1, 6)$

    (D) $(-4, -5)$ (E) $(0, 6)$

---

14. Clean-Ex Unlimited has a spring cleaning special. They charge $60 to clean the carpets in 3 rooms, plus $25 for each additional room. They will clean any size sofa for $35. The cost of cleaning which of the following would be the least?

    (A) 3 rooms, 3 sofas

    (B) 4 rooms, 3 sofas

    (C) 4 rooms, 2 sofas

    (D) 5 rooms, 2 sofas

    (E) 5 rooms, 1 sofa

X		X
	O	
X		O

15. Either an X or an O is to be put in each empty square to complete the grid above. If each row, column, and diagonal containing 3 squares must contain at least one X and at least one O, what is the total number of additional X's that must be used to complete the grid?

    (A) None (B) One (C) Two (D) Three

    (E) Four

Questions 16–32 each consist of two quantities, one in Column A and one in Column B. You are to compare the two quantities and on the answer sheet blacken oval

A if the quantity in Column A is greater;
B if the quantity in Column B is greater;
C if the two quantities are equal;
D if the relationship cannot be determined from the information given.

Notes:
1. In certain questions, information concerning one or both of the quantities to be compared is centered above the two columns.
2. In a given question, a symbol that appears in both columns represents the same thing in Column A as it does in Column B.
3. Letters such as x, n, and k stand for real numbers.

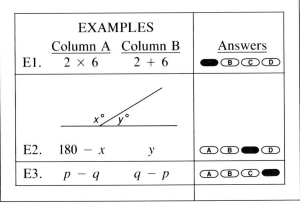

Column A   Column B

$$xyz = 0$$
$$x = 1$$

16.   1 yz

$$a + 17 + c + 23 = 54$$

17. a c

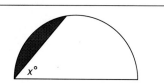

18. Area of shaded region   Area of shaded region
    of semicircle if $x = 45$ of semicircle if $x = 50$

19. $x^2 - y^2$ $y^2 - x^2$

20. $\dfrac{3 \cdot 4 \cdot 5 \cdot 6}{9}$ $\dfrac{2 \cdot 2 \cdot 2 \cdot 3 \cdot 3 \cdot 5}{9}$

21. $\left(\dfrac{1}{2}\right)^3$ $(0.5)^2$

Column A	Column B

22. The product of a   The sum of any integer
    nonzero number and   and its negative
    its reciprocal

$$4X3$$
$$+258$$
$$\overline{7Y1}$$

In the addition problem above, X and Y
represent missing digits.

23. $6 + X$ 9

$$0 < x < y$$

24. x $\dfrac{1}{2}y$

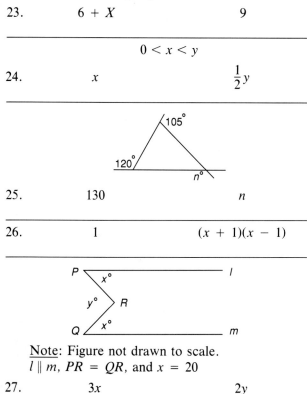

25.   130 n

26.   1 $(x + 1)(x - 1)$

<u>Note</u>: Figure not drawn to scale.
$l \parallel m$, $PR = QR$, and $x = 20$

27. $3x$ $2y$

Suppose there are 10 balls in a bag. All are the
same size. Five are red and 5 are blue. You
select one ball from the bag at random.

28. The probability that   The probability that
    the ball you pick will   the ball you pick will
    be blue   be red

Column A	Column B

Questions 29–30 refer to the following diagram;
x and y are points on the number line.

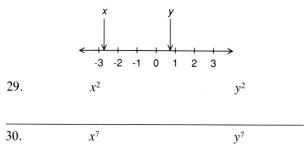

29. x^2 y^2

30. x^7 y^7

The operation $\circ$ is defined by the equation
$x \circ y = x^2 + y^2$.

$$ab \neq 0$$

31. $(a \circ b)^2$ $a^2 \circ b^2$

The price of a certain book is equal to $0.80
more than $\dfrac{8}{10}$ of its price.

32. The price of the book $4.00

Solve each of the remaining problems in this
section using any available space for
scratchwork. Then decide which is the best of
the choices given and blacken the
corresponding oval on the answer sheet.

33. Three musicians in a band receive royalties on
    their records in the ratio of 5:3:2. One year the
    musician receiving the most royalty got $7200.
    What were the total royalties that year?
    (A) $1440   (B) $7200   (C) $10,080

    (D) $11,520   (E) $14,400

34. If $5x = 12$ and $3y = 5$, then $15xy =$
    (A) 17   (B) 60   (C) 36   (D) $\dfrac{25}{12}$ (E) 22

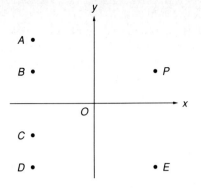

35. In the coordinate plane above, if point P has coordinates $(4, y)$, which lettered point best represents $(-4, 2y)$?

(A) A (B) B (C) C (D) D (E) E

X—	$15.00
Y—	$25.00
Z—	$10.00
	$50.00
Tax +	0.80
	$50.80

36. On the cash register tape above, only item Z was taxed. What was the tax rate?

(A) 0.4%   (B) 0.8%   (C) 4%   (D) 5%

(E) 8%

---

37. A square with perimeter 40 is equal in area to a triangle with base 25. What is the height of the triangle?

(A) 4   (B) 8   (C) 10   (D) 16   (E) 25

---

38. In a school $\frac{2}{3}$ of the students take math classes. One fourth of those students taking math classes take a computer class. What part of the students take both a math and a computer class?

(A) $\frac{1}{6}$ (B) $\frac{1}{4}$ (C) $\frac{3}{7}$ (D) $\frac{2}{3}$ (E) $\frac{11}{12}$

---

39. $(x + y)^2 - 4xy =$

(A) $x^2 - 4xy + y^2$

(B) $(x - y)^2$

(C) $(x - 2y)^2$

(D) $(x + y)^2$

(E) $(x + 2y)^2$

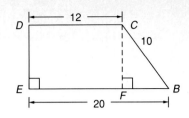

40. In the figure above, find the area of the rectangle *CDEF*.

(A) 240   (B) 96   (C) 120   (D) 48   (E) 72

---

41. If $> n <$ means that both $n - 1$ and $n + 1$ are prime numbers, then which of the following is correct?

(A) $> 20 <$

(B) $> 22 <$

(C) $> 26 <$

(D) $> 28 <$

(E) $> 30 <$

---

42. The value of $\dfrac{\frac{2}{3} + \frac{4}{5}}{\frac{6}{7}}$ can be doubled by doubling the

(A) 2   (B) 4   (C) 5   (D) 6   (E) 7

| 1 fub = 2 gabs |
| 3 fubs = 5 jibs |

43. If fubs, gabs, and jibs are related as shown above, what is the least whole number of jibs that is greater than the sum of 2 fubs and 1 gab?

(A) 1   (B) 3   (C) 5   (D) 7   (E) 12

---

44. If the product of three numbers is an integer, which of the following could be true?

I. None of the three numbers is an integer.
II. Exactly one of the three numbers is an integer.
III. Exactly two of the three numbers are integers.

(A) I only   (B) II only   (C) III only
(D) I and II only   (E) I, II, and III

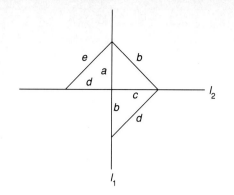

Note: Figure not drawn to scale.

45. In the figure above, if $l_1 \perp l_2$, which of the following is the greatest?

(A) a (B) b (C) c (D) d (E) e

46. How many 3 in. × 3 in. square tiles will fit on a 6 ft × 8 ft rectangular floor?

(A) $5\frac{1}{3}$ (B) 64 (C) 576 (D) 768 (E) 1024

47. How many rectangles with area 36 can be drawn such that all lengths and widths are whole numbers and no two rectangles have the same perimeter?

(A) Six (B) Five (C) Four (D) Three

(E) Two

1, 1, 2, 3, 5, 8, . . .

48. In the sequence above, each term, beginning with the third term 2, is equal to the sum of the two preceding terms. Which of the following terms is an odd integer?

(A) 18th (B) 54th (C) 111th (D) 484th

(E) 966th

49. What is the minimum amount of money that must be invested at 8% simple interest to earn d dollars in interest in a year?

(A) $\dfrac{d}{0.08}$

(B) $0.08d$

(C) $1.08d$

(D) $\dfrac{0.08}{d}$

(E) It cannot be determined from the information given.

50. The average (arithmetic mean) of a certain set of n numbers is 5 percent of the sum of those n numbers. If this average is nonzero, what is the value of n?

(A) 5 (B) 10 (C) 20 (D) 95

(E) It cannot be determined from the information given.

STOP
IF YOU FINISH BEFORE TIME IS CALLED, YOU MAY CHECK YOUR WORK ON THIS SECTION ONLY. DO NOT WORK ON ANY OTHER SECTION.

Exam 2

Time—50 minutes
50 Questions

In this section solve each problem, using any available space on the page for scratchwork. Then decide which is the best of the choices given and blacken the corresponding oval on the answer sheet.

The following information is for your reference in solving some of the problems.

Circle of radius *r:*
Area = πr^2
Circumference = $2\pi r$
The number of degrees of arc in a circle is 360.

The measure in degrees of a straight angle is 180.

Triangle:
The sum of the measures in degrees of the angles of a triangle is 180.

If $\angle CDA$ is a right angle, then

(1) area of $\triangle ABC = \dfrac{AB \times CD}{2}$

(2) $AC^2 = AD^2 + DC^2$

Definitions of symbols:
= is equal to   ≧ is greater than or
≠ is unequal to   equal to
< is less than   ‖ is parallel to
> is greater than   ⊥ is perpendicular
≦ is less than or   to
   equal to

Note: Figures that accompany problems in this test are intended to provide information useful in solving the problems. They are drawn as accurately as possible EXCEPT when it is stated in a specific problem that its figure is not drawn to scale. All figures lie in a plane unless otherwise indicated. All numbers used are real numbers.

1. If $x + 2 = 16 - x$, then $x =$
   (A) 9   (B) −9   (C) 7   (D) 14   (E) −7

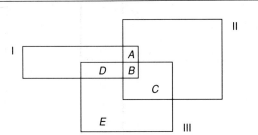

2. In the figure above, which lettered region is common to rectangles I and III, but not part of II?
   (A) *A*   (B) *B*   (C) *C*   (D) *D*   (E) *E*

---

3. How many 50¢ greeting cards can be purchased for *D* dollars?
   (A) $2D$ (B) $\dfrac{D}{50}$ (C) D (D) $50D$ (E) $5D$

---

4. What is the greatest integer that is a factor of 510, 1500, and 1200?
   (A) 2   (B) 10   (C) 5   (D) 30   (E) 102,000

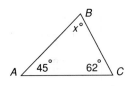

5. In $\triangle ABC$ above, what is the value of *x*?
   (A) 62   (B) 28   (C) 118   (D) 73   (E) 83

---

6. How much will you save by paying $215 cash for a scooter rather than paying $50 down and 6 monthly payments of $37 each?
   (A) $50   (B) $7   (C) $67   (D) $57   (E) $37

---

7. $-(3)(-5)(-6)(-7)$ is equal to which of the following expressions?
   (A) $-3 + 5 + 6 + 7$

   (B) $-3 - 5 - 6 - 7$

   (C) $-3 \cdot 5 \cdot 6 \cdot 7$

   (D) $3(-5)(-6)(-7)$

   (E) $(-3)(-5)(-6)(-7)$

---

8. If $\left(p + \dfrac{2}{3}\right) + \left(p - \dfrac{2}{3}\right) = 5$, then $p =$
   (A) $\dfrac{2}{5}$ (B) $\dfrac{5}{2}$ (C) $\dfrac{7}{3}$ (D) $\dfrac{49}{9}$ (E) $\dfrac{11}{6}$

---

9. 21 is $\dfrac{5}{7}$ of what number?

   (A) 15   (B) $29\dfrac{2}{5}$ (C) 142   (D) 98   (E) $\dfrac{26}{7}$

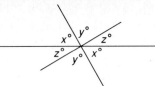

10. In the figure above, if $x = 2z$, and $y = 3z$, then $y =$

(A) 30   (B) 90   (C) 60   (D) 80   (E) 10

Questions 11–12 refer to the following definition.

For all $a, b, c,$ and d such that $ad \neq bc$,

$$\frac{a \,|\, b}{c \,|\, d} = \frac{ab - cd}{ad - bc}.$$

11. $\dfrac{-2 \,|\, 5}{-5 \,|\, 2} =$

(A) 0   (B) $\dfrac{20}{21}$ (C) $-\dfrac{20}{21}$ (D) $\dfrac{5}{7}$ (E) $-\dfrac{5}{7}$

---

12. $\dfrac{\dfrac{-1 \,|\, -1}{-1 \,|\, 2} \,\bigg|\, -1}{-1 \qquad\,|\, 2} =$

(A) -1 (B) 1   (C) 0   (D) 2   (E) -2

---

13. A line segment has endpoints $(3, -5)$ and $(-2, 6)$. What are the coordinates of the midpoint?

(A) $(1, -11)$ (B) $(5, -11)$ (C) $\left(\dfrac{1}{2}, \dfrac{1}{2}\right)$

(D) $\left(-\dfrac{1}{2}, -\dfrac{1}{2}\right)$ (E) $\left(\dfrac{5}{2}, -\dfrac{11}{2}\right)$

---

14. The Print Quick Shop will print the first 100 invitations for $155, plus $67 for each additional 100. They charge $70 per hundred to engrave napkins. The cost of which printing job would be least?

(A) 300 invitations, 300 napkins

(B) 400 invitations, 200 napkins

(C) 500 invitations, 100 napkins

(D) 400 invitations, 300 napkins

(E) 500 invitations, 200 napkins

---

15. Either an X or an O is to be put in each empty square to complete the grid above. If each row, column, and diagonal containing 3 squares must contain at least one X and one O, what is the total number of additional O's that must be used to complete the grid?

(A) None   (B) One   (C) Two   (D) Three

(E) Four

Questions 16–32 each consist of two quantities, one in Column A and one in Column B. You are to compare the two quantities and on the answer sheet blacken oval

A if the quantity in Column A is greater;
B if the quantity in Column B is greater;
C if the two quantities are equal;
D if the relationship cannot be determined from the information given.

Notes:
1. In certain questions, information concerning one or both of the quantities to be compared is centered above the two columns.
2. In a given question, a symbol that appears in both columns represents the same thing in Column A as it does in Column B.
3. Letters such as x, n, and k stand for real numbers.

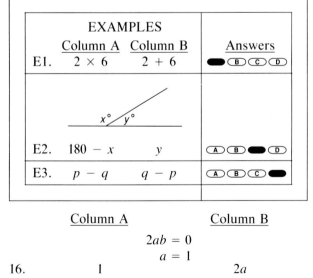

Column A	Column B
$2ab = 0$	
$a = 1$	
16. 1	$2a$

17.
$$a + 16 + c + 27 = 65$$

	a		c

18. Area of shaded region of rectangle if $x = 60$ | Area of shaded region of rectangle if $x = 50$

19. $x^3 - 2y$ | $2y - x^3$

20. $\dfrac{1 \cdot 2 \cdot 3 \cdot 4}{6}$ | $\dfrac{2 \cdot 2 \cdot 2 \cdot 3}{6}$

21. $\left(\dfrac{1}{4}\right)^3$ | $(0.25)^3$

22. The product of a number and its additive inverse | The sum of a nonzero number and its reciprocal

Column A	Column B

$$\begin{array}{r} 2X5 \\ +236 \\ \hline 4Y1 \end{array}$$

In the addition problem above, X and Y represent missing digits.

23. $X + 4$ | 10

$$x < y < 0$$

24. x | $\dfrac{1}{2}y$

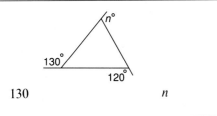

25. 130 | n

26. x^2 | $(x + 1)(x - 1)$

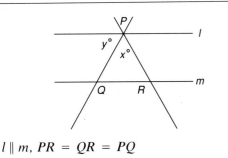

$l \parallel m,\ PR = QR = PQ$

27. x | y

Suppose there are 12 tokens in a bag. All are the same size. Four are red, 4 are blue, and 4 are white.

28. The probability you will draw a red token | The probability you will not draw a red or blue token

Questions 29–30 refer to the following diagram; x and y are points on the number line.

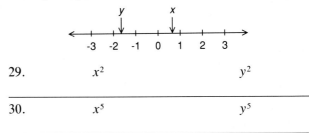

29. x^2 | y^2

30. x^5 | y^5

Column A	Column B

The operation $\circ$ is defined by the equation $x \circ y = x^2 - y^2$.

$$ab \neq 0$$

31. $(a \circ b)^2$ | $a^2 \circ b^2$

The price of a certain scarf is equal to \$0.75 more than $\dfrac{3}{4}$ of its price.

32. The price of the scarf | \$1.00

Solve each of the remaining problems in this section using any available space for scratchwork. Then decide which is the best of the choices given and blacken the corresponding oval on the answer sheet.

---

33. A farmer planted corn, wheat, and soybeans in a ratio of 3:4:2. If he planted 32 acres of wheat, how many acres did he plant in all?

   (A) 24   (B) 16   (C) 40   (D) 72   (E) 288

34. If $6x = 5$ and $7y = 6$, then $42xy =$

   (A) 11   (B) 30   (C) 35   (D) $\dfrac{36}{35}$ (E) 36

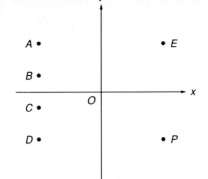

35. In the coordinate plane above, if point P has coordinates $(+6, -y)$, which point best represents $\left(-6, \frac{1}{2}y\right)$?

(A) A　(B) B　(C) C　(D) D　(E) E

| X— $15.00 |
| Y— $35.00 |
| Z— $25.00 |
| $75.00 |
| Tax + 2.45 |
| $77.45 |

36. On the cash register tape above, only item Y was taxed. What was the tax rate?

(A) 7%　(B) 0.7%　(C) 9%　(D) 5%

(E) 0.9%

---

37. A rectangle with an area of 30 is equal in area to a triangle with height of 15. What is the base of the triangle?

(A) 2　(B) 15　(C) 4　(D) 45　(E) $\frac{45}{2}$

---

38. Brad ate $\frac{1}{4}$ of a box of raisins. Mari ate $\frac{2}{3}$ of the remaining raisins. What part of the box did Mari eat?

(A) $\frac{2}{3}$　(B) $\frac{1}{6}$　(C) $\frac{1}{2}$　(D) $\frac{8}{3}$　(E) $\frac{11}{12}$

---

39. $(x - y)^2 + 2xy =$

(A) $x^2 + 2xy - y^2$

(B) $x^2 + 2xy + y^2$

(C) $x^2 - y^2$

(D) $x^2 + y^2$

(E) $(x - 2y)^2$

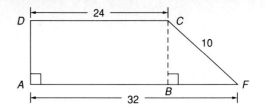

40. In the figure above, find the area of the rectangle $ABCD$.

(A) 240　(B) 320　(C) 256　(D) 192

(E) 144

---

41. If $<n>$ means both $n - 1$ and $n + 1$ are composite numbers, then which of the following is incorrect?

(A) $<9>$

(B) $<10>$

(C) $<13>$

(D) $<17>$

(E) $<50>$

---

42. The value of $\dfrac{\frac{2}{5} + \frac{3}{7}}{\frac{6}{11}}$ can be halved by doubling the

(A) 2　(B) 6　(C) 7　(D) 11　(E) 5

$$1 \text{ wid} = 3 \text{ gads}$$
$$4 \text{ wids} = 7 \text{ ligs}$$

43. If wids, gads, and ligs are related as shown above, what is the least whole number of ligs that is greater than the sum of 3 wids and 2 gads?

(A) 6　(B) 7　(C) 5　(D) 8　(E) 1

---

44. If the sum of three numbers is an integer, which of the following could be true?

　I. None of the three numbers is an integer.
　II. Exactly one of the three numbers is an integer.
　III. Exactly two of the three numbers are integers.

(A) I only　(B) II only　(C) III only

(D) I and II only　(E) I, II, and III

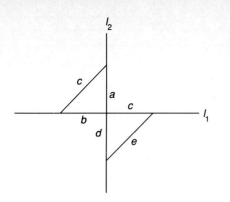

Note: Figure not drawn to scale.

45. In the figure above, if $l_1 \perp l_2$, which of the following is the greatest?

(A) a (B) b (C) c (D) d (E) e

---

46. How many 6 in. × 6 in. square tiles will fit on a square floor with 12-ft sides?

(A) 3 (B) 72 (C) 36 (D) 72 (E) 576

---

47. How many rectangles with area 24 can be drawn such that all lengths and widths are whole numbers and no two rectangles have the same perimeter?

(A) One (B) Two (C) Three (D) Four

(E) Five

3, 3, 6, 9, 15, 24, . . .

48. In the sequence above, each term, beginning with the third term 6, is equal to the sum of the two preceding terms. Which of the following terms is an even integer?

(A) 18th (B) 53rd (C) 110th (D) 484th

(E) 901st

---

49. How many hours would it take to travel d miles at a speed of 50 mi/h?

(A) $50d$

(B) $\dfrac{50}{d}$

(C) $\dfrac{d}{50}$

(D) $d + 50$

(E) It cannot be determined from the information given.

---

50. The average (arithmetic mean) of a set of n numbers is 10% of the sum of those n numbers. If the average is nonzero, what is the value of n?

(A) 5 (B) 10 (C) 20 (D) 30

(E) It cannot be determined from the information given.

STOP

IF YOU FINISH BEFORE TIME IS CALLED, YOU MAY CHECK YOUR WORK ON THIS SECTION ONLY. DO NOT WORK ON ANY OTHER SECTION.

In this section solve each problem, using any available space on the page for scratchwork. Then decide which is the best of the choices given and blacken the corresponding oval on the answer sheet.

The following information is for your reference in solving some of the problems.

Circle of radius r:
Area $= \pi r^2$
Circumference $= 2\pi r$
The number of degrees of arc in a circle is 360.

The measure in degrees of a straight angle is 180.

Triangle:
The sum of the measures in degrees of the angles of a triangle is 180.

If $\angle CDA$ is a right angle, then

(1) area of $\triangle ABC = \dfrac{AB \times CD}{2}$

(2) $AC^2 = AD^2 + DC^2$

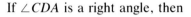

Definitions of symbols:
$=$ is equal to
$\neq$ is unequal to
$<$ is less than
$>$ is greater than
$\leq$ is less than or equal to

$\geq$ is greater than or equal to
$\parallel$ is parallel to
$\perp$ is perpendicular to

Note: Figures that accompany problems in this test are intended to provide information useful in solving the problems. They are drawn as accurately as possible EXCEPT when it is stated in a specific problem that its figure is not drawn to scale. All figures lie in a plane unless otherwise indicated. All numbers used are real numbers.

1. If $7 - x = x - 13$, then $x =$
   (A) 6   (B) 20   (C) 10   (D) -10 (E) -6

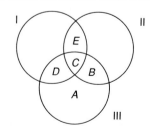

2. In the figure above, which lettered region is common to circles I and III, but not part of II?
   (A) A (B) B (C) C (D) D (E) E

3. How many 22¢ stamps can be purchased with c cents?
   (A) $\dfrac{22}{c}$ (B) $\dfrac{c}{22}$ (C) $\dfrac{c}{2.2}$ (D) $22c$
   (E) $0.22c$

4. What is the least common multiple of 6, 15, and 14?
   (A) 30   (B) 1260   (C) 1   (D) 210   (E) 84

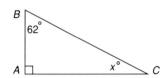

5. In $\triangle ABC$ above, what is the value of x?
   (A) 62   (B) 28   (C) 118   (D) 90   (E) 38

6. How much can be saved by buying a bedroom set for $1300 in cash rather than paying $100 down and 12 monthly payments of $125 each?
   (A) $200   (B) $400   (C) $300   (D) $225
   (E) $52

7. $-(2 - 4)(-3)$ is equal to which of the following expressions?
   (A) $(-2 + 4)(3)$

   (B) $(2 + 4)(-3)$

   (C) $(-2 - 4)(-3)$

   (D) $(2 - 4)(3)$

   (E) $(4 - 2)(3)$

8. If $\left(r + \dfrac{1}{4}\right) + \left(r - \dfrac{1}{4}\right) = 7$, then $r =$
   (A) $\dfrac{7}{2}$ (B) $\dfrac{2}{7}$ (C) $\dfrac{113}{4}$ (D) 7   (E) $\dfrac{13}{4}$

9. 48 is $\dfrac{5}{6}$ of what number?
   (A) $57\dfrac{3}{5}$ (B) 40   (C) 8   (D) $9\dfrac{3}{5}$ (E) $48\dfrac{5}{6}$

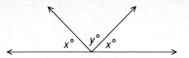

10. In the figure above, if $y = 2x$, then $x =$

    (A) 45   (B) 90   (C) 60   (D) 180   (E) $4\frac{1}{2}$

Questions 11–12 refer to the following definition.

For all a and b, $a * b = 2b - a$.

11. $3 * 7 =$

    (A) 21   (B) -1 (C) 11   (D) 17   (E) 10

---

12. $-1 * 1 =$

    (A) -1 (B) 3   (C) 1   (D) 0   (E) 2

---

13. A line segment has endpoints $(-6, 2)$ and $(-2, -4)$. What are the coordinates of the midpoint?

    (A) $(-8, -2)$ (B) $(-4, -1)$ (C) $(-2, 3)$

    (D) $(-4, 6)$ (E) $(-5, 0)$

---

14. Speedy Rental Cars charges $45 a day with unlimited mileage or $20 a day and $0.12 per mile. If you are going to rent the car for 3 days and drive 150 miles, what will be the least possible cost?

    (A) $135   (B) $78   (C) $38   (D) $60

    (E) $18

B		B
	A	
B		A

15. Either an A or a B is to be put in each empty square to complete the grid above. If each row, column, and diagonal containing 3 squares must contain at least one A and one B, what is the total number of additional A's that must be used to complete the grid?

    (A) One   (B) Two   (C) Three   (D) Four

    (E) Five

Questions 16–32 each consist of two quantities, one in Column A and one in Column B. You are to compare the two quantities and on the answer sheet blacken oval

A if the quantity in Column A is greater;
B if the quantity in Column B is greater;
C if the two quantities are equal;
D if the relationship cannot be determined from the information given.

Notes:
1. In certain questions, information concerning one or both of the quantities to be compared is centered above the two columns.
2. In a given question, a symbol that appears in both columns represents the same thing in Column A as it does in Column B.
3. Letters such as x, n, and k stand for real numbers.

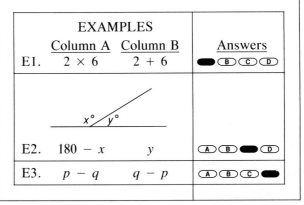

EXAMPLES		
Column A	Column B	Answers
E1. 2×6	$2 + 6$	●ⒷⒸⒹ
E2. $180 - x$	y	ⒶⒷ●Ⓓ
E3. $p - q$	$q - p$	ⒶⒷⒸ●

          Column A   Column B

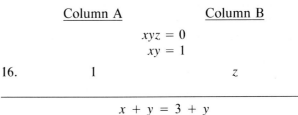

$$xyz = 0$$
$$xy = 1$$

16.   1 z

$$x + y = 3 + y$$

17. x y

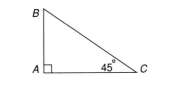

Note: Figure not drawn to scale.

18. AB AC

	Column A	Column B
19.	a	$-a$
20.	$\dfrac{2\cdot3\cdot4\cdot6}{7}$	$\dfrac{2\cdot2\cdot2\cdot2\cdot3\cdot3}{7}$

	Column A	Column B
21.	$\left(\dfrac{1}{8}\right)^3$	$(0.125)^2$
22.	ab	$(-a)(-b)$

$$
\begin{array}{r}
2X7 \\
+369 \\
\hline
6Y6
\end{array}
$$

In the addition problem above, X and Y represent missing digits.

	Column A	Column B
23.	$6 + X$	8

$$0 < x < y$$

24.	$-x$	$-y$

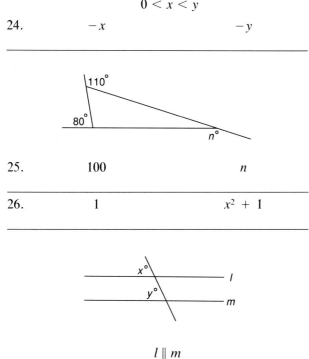

25.	100	n
26.	1	$x^2 + 1$

$$l \parallel m$$

27.	x	y

Suppose there are 10 marbles in a bag. All are the same size. Seven are red and three are blue. You select a marble from the bag at random.

28.	The probability the marble is red.	The probability the marble is not blue.

Questions 29–30 refer to the following diagram; a and b are points on the number line.

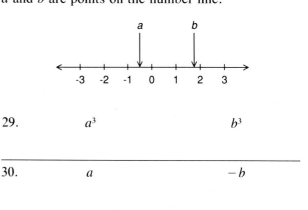

	Column A	Column B
29.	a^3	b^3
30.	a	$-b$

The operation * is defined by the equation $x * y = x^2 + y^4$.

$$ab \neq 0$$

31.	$(a * b)^2$	$a^2 * b^2$

The price of a certain pen is equal to \$0.90 more than $\dfrac{7}{10}$ of its price.

32.	The price of the pen	\$3.00

Solve each of the remaining problems in this section using any available space for scratchwork. Then decide which is the best of the choices given and blacken the corresponding oval on the answer sheet.

33. Benjamin, Amanda, and Kim own a business. They split their profits in the ratio of 4:3:2. One month Benjamin received \$2300 in profits. What were the total profits that month?

   (A) \$5175   (B) \$1725   (C) \$1150

   (D) \$9555   (E) \$20,700

34. If $2x = 17$ and $4y = 11$, then $8xy =$

   (A) 28   (B) 187   (C) 68   (D) $\dfrac{22}{17}$ (E) 22

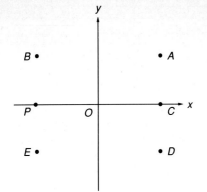

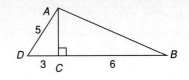

35. In the coordinate plane above, if point P has coordinates $(-x, 0)$, which point best represents $(x, -2)$?

(A) A   (B) B   (C) C   (D) D   (E) E

```
X—$15.00
Y—$25.00
Z—$10.00
  $50.00
Tax + 2.80
  $52.80
```

36. On the cash register tape above, items X and Y were taxed. What was the tax rate?

(A) .7%   (B) $9\frac{1}{3}$%   (C) 7%   (D) .093%

(E) 14.28%

---

37. A square with sides equal to 8 has the same area as a triangle whose base is 16. What is the height of the triangle?

(A) 2   (B) 4   (C) 8   (D) 16   (E) 32

---

38. Pat ate $\frac{1}{3}$ of the pizza. Nicole ate $\frac{1}{2}$ of the remaining pizza. What part of the pizza did Nicole eat?

(A) $\frac{1}{6}$ (B) $\frac{5}{6}$ (C) $\frac{2}{3}$ (D) $\frac{2}{5}$ (E) $\frac{1}{3}$

---

39. $(a - b)^2 + 4ab =$

(A) $a^2 + 4ab - b^2$

(B) $(a + b)^2$

(C) $(a - 2b)^2$

(D) $(a - b)^2$

(E) $(a + 2b)^2$

---

40. In the figure above, find the area of $\triangle ABC$.

(A) 6   (B) 12   (C) $22\frac{1}{2}$ (D) 24   (E) 51

(A) 51   (B) 57   (C) 63

41. Which of the numbers above are prime?

(A) A   (B) B   (C) C   (D) A and B

(E) None

---

42. The value of $\dfrac{\frac{1}{2} + \frac{4}{3}}{\frac{5}{7}}$ can be tripled by tripling the

(A) 1   (B) 3   (C) 5   (D) 7   (E) 4

$$a = 2b$$
$$3b = 5c$$

43. Which of the following shows the relationship between a and c?

(A) $3a = 10c$ (B) $a = 6c$ (C) $a = 10c$

(D) $15c = 2a$ (E) $5c = 2a$

---

44. If the product of two nonzero numbers is an integer, which of the following could be true?

I. Neither number is an integer.
II. Exactly one of the numbers is an integer.
III. Both of the numbers are proper fractions.

(A) I only   (B) II only   (C) III only
(D) I and II only   (E) I, II, and III

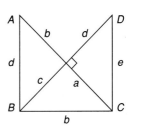

Note: Figure not drawn to scale.

45. In the figure $AC \perp BD$. Which of the following is the greatest?

(A) a (B) b (C) c (D) d (E) e

---

46. How many 5 cm × 5 cm square tiles will fit on a rectangular floor that is 6 m × 7 m?

(A) 16,800   (B) $1\frac{17}{25}$ (C) 1050

(D) $16\frac{4}{5}$ (E) $4\frac{1}{5}$

47. How many rectangles with area 32 can be drawn such that all lengths and widths are whole numbers and no two rectangles have the same perimeter?

(A) Six   (B) Five   (C) Four   (D) Three

(E) Two

2, 5, 10, 17, 26, . . .

48. What is the tenth term of the sequence above?

(A) 100   (B) 29   (C) 101   (D) 190

(E) 1001

49. What is the minimum speed one can drive to go m miles in 3 hours?

(A) $3m$ (B) $\frac{3}{m}$ (C) $\frac{m}{3}$

(D) $m + 3$ (E) $m - 3$

50. The average (arithmetic mean) of a certain set of n numbers is 4 percent of the sum of those n numbers. If their average is nonzero, what is the value of n?

(A) 4   (B) 8   (C) 25   (D) 96

(E) It cannot be determined from the information given.

STOP
IF YOU FINISH BEFORE TIME IS CALLED, YOU MAY CHECK YOUR WORK ON THIS SECTION ONLY. DO NOT WORK ON ANY OTHER SECTION.

In this section solve each problem, using any available space on the page for scratchwork. Then decide which is the best of the choices given and blacken the corresponding oval on the answer sheet.

The following information is for your reference in solving some of the problems.

Circle of radius r:
Area $= \pi r^2$
Circumference $= 2\pi r$
The number of degress of arc in a circle is 360.

The measure in degrees of a straight angle is 180.

Triangle:
The sum of the measures in degrees of the angles of a triangle is 180.

If $\angle CDA$ is a right angle, then

(1) area of $\triangle ABC = \dfrac{AB \times CD}{2}$

(2) $AC^2 = AD^2 + DC^2$

Definitions of symbols:
$=$ is equal to	$\geqq$ is greater than or equal to
$\neq$ is unequal to	
$<$ is less than	$\parallel$ is parallel to
$>$ is greater than	$\perp$ is perpendicular to
$\leqq$ is less than or equal to	

<u>Note</u>: Figures that accompany problems in this test are intended to provide information useful in solving the problems. They are drawn as accurately as possible EXCEPT when it is stated in a specific problem that its figure is not drawn to scale. All figures lie in a plane unless otherwise indicated. All numbers used are real numbers.

1. Which of the following numbers is <u>not</u> an integral multiple of 8?

    (A) 8 (B) 0 (C) 4 (D) 16 (E) -8

---

2. In a recent survey, the results showed that 50 people use Product A, 30 use Product B, and 10 use both Product A and Product B. How many people participated in the survey?

    (A) 90 (B) 70 (C) 80 (D) 100 (E) 50

---

3. Twenty-nine less than twice forty equals

    (A) 11 (B) 61 (C) 109 (D) 51 (E) 69

---

4. For which of the following values is $\dfrac{5}{x}$ undefined?

    (A) 1 (B) -5 (C) -1 (D) 0 (E) 5

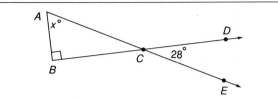

5. In the diagram above, what is the value of x?

    (A) 28 (B) 90 (C) 62 (D) 72 (E) 152

---

6. How many hours are in a week?

    (A) 24 (B) 168 (C) 120 (D) 84 (E) 60

---

7. $(x + y) - (x - y) =$

    (A) 0 (B) $x^2 - y^2$ (C) $2x$ (D) $2y$

    (E) $2x + 2y$

---

8. If $2x - 3 = 6$, then $x =$

    (A) 9 (B) 3 (C) $\dfrac{9}{2}$ (D) $\dfrac{2}{9}$ (E) $\dfrac{3}{2}$

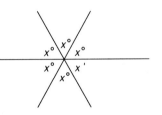

9. If six line segments meet at a point as shown in the figure above, then $x =$

    (A) 30 (B) 60 (C) 40 (D) 72 (E) 45

---

10. A restaurant owner has calculated that it takes $\dfrac{2}{3}$ pound of rice to make enough to serve 10 people. How much rice will be needed to serve 50 people?

    (A) $33\dfrac{1}{3}$ (B) $3\dfrac{1}{3}$ (C) 3 (D) $6\dfrac{2}{3}$ (E) $7\dfrac{1}{2}$

Questions 11–12 refer to the following definition.

For all m, n, r, and t such that $mr \neq nt$,

$$\frac{m \mid n}{r \mid t} = \frac{mn - rt}{mr - nt}.$$

11. $\dfrac{3 \mid 2}{-3 \mid 2} =$

    (A) $-\dfrac{12}{13}$ (B) 0 (C) $-\dfrac{12}{4}$ (D) -1 (E) 1

---

12. 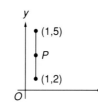 $=$

    (A) 1 (B) -1 (C) 0 (D) 2 (E) -2

---

13. In the figure above, what are the coordinates of point P if P is the midpoint of the segment?

    (A) $(2, 4)$ (B) $\left(1, \dfrac{3}{2}\right)$ (C) $(-1, -3)$

    (D) $\left(1, \dfrac{7}{2}\right)$ (E) $(2, 7)$

---

14. Flat sheets cost $7.50. Fitted sheets cost $9.50. A set of pillow cases cost $5.25. The charges for which of the following would be the least?

    (A) 2 flat sheets, 1 set of pillow cases

    (B) 1 flat sheet, 1 fitted sheet, 1 set of pillow cases

    (C) 1 fitted sheet, 1 set of pillow cases

    (D) 1 flat sheet, 1 fitted sheet

    (E) 1 flat sheet, 2 sets of pillowcases

---

15. Four people are taking turns moving in a game. A moves first, B moves second, C moves third, and D moves fourth. After 15 moves, whose turn is it?

    (A) A   (B) B   (C) C   (D) D

    (E) It cannot be determined from the information given.

Questions 16–32 each consist of two quantities, one in Column A and one in Column B. You are to compare the two quantities and on the answer sheet blacken oval

A if the quantity in Column A is greater;
B if the quantity in Column B is greater;
C if the two quantities are equal;
D if the relationship cannot be determined from the information given.

Notes:
1. In certain questions, information concerning one or both of the quantities to be compared is centered above the two columns.
2. In a given question, a symbol that appears in both columns represents the same thing in Column A as it does in Column B.
3. Letters such as x, n, and k stand for real numbers.

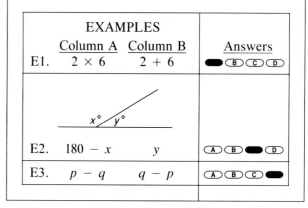

EXAMPLES		
Column A	Column B	Answers
E1. 2×6	$2 + 6$	●BCD
E2. $180 - x$	y	AB●D
E3. $p - q$	$q - p$	ABC●

      Column A   Column B

$$AB = 1$$

16. B $\dfrac{1}{A}$

---

17. 2^4 8

---

18. length of AB π

      Column A   Column B

$$16 = 9 + x + 7 - y$$

19. x y

$$xy \neq 0$$

20. $(x - y)(x + y)$ x^2

$\triangle ABC$ has angles measuring $a°$, $b°$, and $c°$, respectively.

21. $a + b + c$ 360

---

22. The product of a nonzero number and the additive inverse of its reciprocal   The sum of any integer and its additive inverse

---

$$\begin{array}{r} 4X3 \\ -258 \\ \hline 2Y5 \end{array}$$

In the subtraction problem above, X and Y represent missing digits.

23. $6 + Y$ 10

---

24. The probability that a day of the week picked at random from the seven days of the week will begin with "T"   The probability that a day of the week picked at random from the seven days of the week will begin with "S"

$l \parallel m$

25. $x + y$ 90

     Column A   Column B

x represents the number of seconds in 5 minutes

26. $\dfrac{x}{5}$ 30

$l \parallel m$, $PQ = QR$, $PR \perp m$, $x = 30$

27. $3x$ $2y$

Let $a, b > 0$

28. $\sqrt{a + b}$ $\sqrt{a} + \sqrt{b}$

---

29. BC $(AB)\sqrt{2}$

$$-3x < 6$$

30. x -2

$$a \neq 0$$

31. a $\dfrac{1}{a}$

---

32. $\dfrac{1}{10}$ 10^{-2}

Solve each of the remaining problems in this section using any available space for scratchwork. Then decide which is the best of the choices given and blacken the corresponding oval on the answer sheet.

33. If x and y are related by the formula $y = \dfrac{k}{x}$, where k is a constant, and $y = 9$ when $x = 3$, then $k =$

(A) 3   (B) $\dfrac{1}{3}$ (C) 27   (D) 12   (E) 6

---

34. If there are 25 red candies and 16 green candies in a bag, what is the ratio of green candies to red candies?

(A) $\dfrac{5}{4}$ (B) $\dfrac{4}{5}$ (C) $\dfrac{25}{16}$ (D) $\dfrac{16}{25}$ (E) $\dfrac{16}{41}$

---

35. The point $(-3, -2)$ lies in which quadrant of the graph above?

(A) I   (B) II   (C) III   (D) IV   (E) 0

36. The sales tax on a $14 purchase is $0.70. What is the tax rate?

   (A) 20%   (B) 2%   (C) .2%   (D) 5%

   (E) .5%

37. If the area of a square is 49 square units, what is the perimeter of the square?

   (A) 7   (B) 14   (C) 21   (D) 28   (E) 196

38. One half of the class is taking algebra, and $\frac{4}{5}$ of those taking algebra are passing. What part of the class is taking algebra and passing?

   (A) $\frac{1}{2}$ (B) $\frac{4}{5}$ (C) $\frac{4}{7}$ (D) $\frac{13}{10}$ (E) $\frac{2}{5}$

39. $(a + b)^2 + (a - b)^2 =$

   (A) $2(a^2 + b^2)$

   (B) a^2

   (C) $a^2 - 4ab + b^2$

   (D) $a^2 + 4ab + b^2$

   (E) $2a^2 + 4ab + 2b^2$

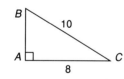

40. In the figure above, what is the area of $\triangle ABC$?

   (A) 40   (B) 80   (C) 48   (D) 24   (E) 30

41. Which of the following numbers is <u>not</u> composite?

   (A) 12   (B) 51   (C) 1   (D) 63   (E) 119

42. The value of $\dfrac{\frac{2}{3} + \frac{4}{5}}{\frac{6}{7}}$ can be halved by doubling the

   (A) 2   (B) 4   (C) 5   (D) 6   (E) 7

43. If $5n = q$ and $4q = d$, then $n =$

   (A) $20d$ (B) $\frac{20}{d}$ (C) $\frac{d}{20}$ (D) $\frac{5}{4}d$ (E) $\frac{4}{5}d$

44. If the product of 5 numbers is positive, which of the following could be true?

   I. None are negative.
   II. None are positive.
   III. The number of positive factors in the product is divisible by 2.

   (A) I only   (B) II only   (C) III only
   (D) I and III only   (E) I, II, and III

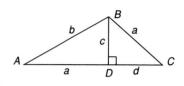

   Note: Figure not drawn to scale.

45. In the figure above, which of the following is the greatest?

   (A) a (B) b (C) c (D) d

   (E) It cannot be determined from the information given.

46. The second hand on a clock rotates around the center how many times as fast as the minute hand?

   (A) 10   (B) 12   (C) 30   (D) 60   (E) 3600

47. How many rectangles with area 18 can be drawn such that all the lengths and widths are whole numbers and no two rectangles have the same perimeter?

   (A) One   (B) Two   (C) Three   (D) Four

   (E) Five

48. 1, 3, 6, 10, 15, 21, . . .

   In the sequence above, the nth term is equal to the sum of the first n integers. Which of the following terms is an even integer?

   (A) 18th   (B) 54th   (C) 113th   (D) 484th

   (E) 966th

49. The price of a coat decreased from a to $(a - b)$. By what percent did the price of the coat decrease?

(A) $100 \times \dfrac{b}{a}$

(B) $100 \times \dfrac{a}{a - b}$

(C) $100 \times \dfrac{a - b}{b}$

(D) $100 \times b$

(E) $100 \times (a - b)$

50. The average weight of a player on the high school football team is 190 lb. If there are 22 players on the team, how much does the team weigh as a group?

(A) 212   (B) 4180   (C) $8\dfrac{7}{11}$ (D) 760

(E) 3180

STOP
IF YOU FINISH BEFORE TIME IS CALLED, YOU MAY CHECK YOUR WORK ON THIS SECTION ONLY. DO NOT WORK ON ANY OTHER SECTION.

College Entrance Exam Solutions

EXAM 1

1. C $x - 3 = 15 - x$
$2x = 18$
$x = 9$

2. E Areas E and C are common to I and II, but only E is also not part of III.

3. D Use a proportion. 10 pencils cost 1 dollar.
$\dfrac{10}{1} = \dfrac{x}{D}$ $10D = x$

4. E $840 = 2 \cdot 2 \cdot 2 \cdot 3 \cdot 5 \cdot 7$
$1200 = 2 \cdot 2 \cdot 2 \cdot 2 \cdot 3 \cdot 5 \cdot 5$
$1400 = 2 \cdot 2 \cdot 2 \cdot 5 \cdot 5 \cdot 7$
$\text{GCF} = 2 \cdot 2 \cdot 2 \cdot 5 = 40$

5. B $90 + 32 + x = 180$
$x = 58$

6. D $20 + 6(31) = 206$
$206 - 185 = 21$

7. E $-(-2)(-3)(-4)(-5) = 2(-3)(-4)(-5)$

8. B $\left(p + \dfrac{1}{2}\right) + \left(p - \dfrac{1}{2}\right) = 3$
$2p = 3$
$p = \dfrac{3}{2}$

9. A $36 = \dfrac{3}{8}x$
$\dfrac{8}{3} \cdot \dfrac{36}{1} = x$
$96 = x$

10. A $4x + 2y = 360$
$4x + x = 360$
$5x = 360$
$x = 72$
$x = 2y = 72, y = 36$

11. C $\dfrac{3 \begin{vmatrix} -2 \\ \end{vmatrix}}{-3 \begin{vmatrix} 2 \end{vmatrix}} = \dfrac{3(-2) - (-3)(2)}{3(-3) - (-2)(2)} =$
$\dfrac{-6 + 6}{-9 + 4} = \dfrac{0}{-5} = 0$

12. D $\dfrac{1 \begin{vmatrix} 1 \\ \end{vmatrix}}{1 \begin{vmatrix} 2 \end{vmatrix}} = \dfrac{1(1) - 1(2)}{1(1) - 1(2)} = \dfrac{-1}{-1} = 1$
$\dfrac{\frac{1 | 1}{1 | 2} \, | \, 1}{1 \, | \, 2} = \dfrac{1 | 1}{1 | 2} = 1$

13. C $\left(\dfrac{-3 + 1}{2}, \dfrac{5 + 7}{2}\right) = (-1, 6)$

14. E A. $60 + 3(35) = \$165$
B. $60 + 25 + 3(35) = \$190$
C. $60 + 25 + 2(35) = \$155$
D. $60 + 2(25) + 2(35) = \$180$
E. $60 + 2(25) + 35 = \$145$

15. C

X	O	X
O	O	X
X	X	O

2 more X's are needed.

16. A $yz = 0$, so $1 > 0$

17. D The values of a and c vary.
$a + c = 14$

18. A $50°$ is greater than $45°$, so when $x = 45$, the shaded area of the semicircle is greater.

19. D If $x = 2$ and $y = 3$,
then $x^2 - y^2 < y^2 - x^2$
If $x = 3$ and $y = 2$,
then $x^2 - y^2 > y^2 - x^2$
If $x = y$, both expressions are zero.

20. C $\dfrac{2 \cdot 2 \cdot 2 \cdot 3 \cdot 3 \cdot 5}{9} = \dfrac{4 \cdot 6 \cdot 3 \cdot 5}{9} =$
$\dfrac{3 \cdot 4 \cdot 5 \cdot 6}{9}$

21. B $\dfrac{1}{2} = 0.5, \left(\dfrac{1}{2}\right)^3 = \dfrac{1}{8}, \left(\dfrac{1}{2}\right)^2 = \dfrac{1}{4}$
$\dfrac{1}{8} < \dfrac{1}{4}$, so $\left(\dfrac{1}{2}\right)^3 < (0.5)^2$

22. A $a \cdot \dfrac{1}{a} = 1, a + -a = 0$
$1 > 0$

23. A $X + 5 + 1 \geq 10$
$X + 6 \geq 10$
$X + 6 > 9$

24. D Let $x = 3$ and $y = 4$.
$3 < 4$ and $3 > \dfrac{1}{2}y$ or $3 > 2$
Let $x = 3$ and $y = 10$.
$3 < 10$ and $3 < \dfrac{1}{2}y$ or $3 < 5$

25. B $180 - 120 = 60$
$180 - 105 = 75$
$60 + 75 = 135$
$180 - 135 = 45$
$n = 180 - 45$
$n = 135$

26. D If $x = 1$, then $(x + 1)(x - 1) = 0$
If $x = 2$ or -2, then
$(x + 1)(x - 1) = 3$

27. B Drop a perpendicular from P to Q. Then in $\triangle PQR$
$y + 2(90 - x) = 180$.
$y = 180 - 2(90 - x)$
$y = 180 - 2(90 - 20)$
$y = 180 - 2(70) = 40$
$3x = 60$ $2y = 80$
$3x < 2y$

28. C $P(blue) = \dfrac{5}{10} = \dfrac{1}{2}$
$P(red) = \dfrac{5}{10} = \dfrac{1}{2}$

29. A $x^2 > 4, y^2 < 1, x^2 > y^2$

30. B $x^7 < 0, y^7 > 0, x^7 < y^7$

31. A $(a \circ b)^2 = (a^2 + b^2)^2$
$= a^4 + 2a^2b^2 + b^4$
$a^2 \circ b^2 = (a^2)^2 + (b^2)^2 = a^4 + b^4$
Since $2a^2b^2 \neq 0$, $(a \circ b)^2 > a^2 \circ b^2$.

32. C $p = \dfrac{8}{10}p + 0.80$
$\dfrac{2}{10}p = 0.80$
$p = 0.80 \cdot \dfrac{10}{2}$
$p = 4$

33. E There is a total of 10 parts, $5 + 3 + 2$.
$\dfrac{5}{10} = \dfrac{7200}{x}$
$5x = 72,000$
$x = \$14,400$

34. B $15xy = 5x \cdot 3y = 12 \cdot 5 = 60$

35. A Since $y > 0$, $(-4, 2y)$ must be in the second quadrant.

36. E $r(10.00) = 0.80$

$r = \dfrac{0.80}{10}$

$r = 0.08$, or 8%

37. B Perimeter of a square is 40; sides are 10.
Area of the square is $10 \cdot 10$, or 100.

Area of the triangle $= 100 = \left(\dfrac{1}{2}\right)25h$

$100 = \dfrac{25}{2}h$

$\dfrac{2}{25} \cdot 100 = h$

$8 = h$

38. A $\dfrac{1}{4}\left(\dfrac{2}{3}\right) = \dfrac{2}{12} = \dfrac{1}{6}$

39. B $(x + y)^2 - 4xy =$
$x^2 + 2xy + y^2 - 4xy =$
$x^2 - 2xy + y^2 =$
$(x - y)^2$

40. E $FB = 20 - 12 = 8$
$10^2 = 8^2 + CF^2$
$100 = 64 + CF^2$
$36 = CF^2$
$6 = CF$

Area $= 12(6) = 72$

41. E 19, 21   no
21, 23   no
25, 27   no
27, 29   no
29, 31   yes

42. E $\dfrac{\frac{2}{3} + \frac{4}{5}}{\frac{6}{7}} = \dfrac{7}{6}\left(\dfrac{2}{3} + \dfrac{4}{5}\right)$

Double the value. The effect is doubling the 7.

$2 \cdot \dfrac{7}{6}\left(\dfrac{2}{3} + \dfrac{4}{5}\right) = \dfrac{14}{6}\left(\dfrac{2}{3} + \dfrac{4}{5}\right)$

43. C 1 fub = 2 gabs, so 1 gab = $\dfrac{1}{2}$ fub

3 fubs = 5 jibs, so 1 fub = $\dfrac{5}{3}$ jib

2 fubs + 1 gab = $\dfrac{5}{2}$ fubs

$\dfrac{5}{2}$ fubs = $\dfrac{5}{2} \cdot \dfrac{5}{3}$ jibs =

$\dfrac{25}{6}$ jibs = $4\dfrac{1}{6}$ jibs

The least whole number of jibs that is greater than 2 fubs and 1 gab is 5 jibs.

44. E All could be true.

(I) $\dfrac{1}{2} \cdot \dfrac{3}{4} \cdot \dfrac{8}{3} = 1$

(II) $6 \cdot \dfrac{1}{2} \cdot \dfrac{1}{3} = 1$

(III) $2 \cdot 3 \cdot \dfrac{1}{6} = 1$

45. E $e > a$
$e > d > b > c$

46. D 6 ft $\times$ 8 ft =
72 in. $\times$ 96 in. = 6912 in.²
3 in. $\times$ 3 in. = 9 in.²
6912 ÷ 9 = 768

47. B 1 × 36, $P = 74$
2 × 18, $P = 40$
3 × 12, $P = 30$
4 × 9, $P = 26$
6 × 6, $P = 24$

48. D Extend the sequence, . . . 13, 21, 34, . . . , and note every 3rd term is even. 18, 54, 111, and 966 are all multiples of 3, thus they are even.

49. A $i = prt$
$d = p(0.08)(1)$

$\dfrac{d}{0.08} = p$

50. C A = average
s = sum

$A = \dfrac{s}{n} = 0.05s = \dfrac{s}{20}$

$\dfrac{s}{n} = \dfrac{s}{20}$

If $s \neq 0$, then $n = 20$.

EXAM 2

1. C $x + 2 = 16 - x$
$2x = 14$
$x = 7$

2. D Areas D and B are common to I and III, but only D is also not part of II.

3. A Use a proportion. 2 cards cost 1 dollar.
$\dfrac{2}{1} = \dfrac{x}{D} \qquad 2D = x$

4. D $510 = 2 \cdot 3 \cdot 5 \cdot 17$
$1500 = 2 \cdot 2 \cdot 3 \cdot 5 \cdot 5 \cdot 5$
$1200 = 2 \cdot 2 \cdot 2 \cdot 2 \cdot 3 \cdot 5 \cdot 5$
GCF $= 2 \cdot 3 \cdot 5 = 30$

5. D $x + 45 + 62 = 180$
$x + 107 = 180$
$x = 73$

6. D $50 + 6(37) = 272$
$272 - 215 = 57$

7. E $-(3)(-5)(-6)(-7) = (-3)(-5)(-6)(-7)$

8. B $\left(p + \dfrac{2}{3}\right) + \left(p - \dfrac{2}{3}\right) = 5$
$2p = 5$
$p = \dfrac{5}{2}$

9. B $21 = \dfrac{5}{7} \cdot x$

$\dfrac{7}{5} \cdot 21 = x$

$\dfrac{147}{5} = x$

$29\dfrac{2}{5} = x$

10. B $360 = x + y + z + z + y + x$
$360 = 2x + 2y + 2z$
$360 = 2(2z) + 2(3z) + 2z$
$360 = 4z + 6z + 2z$
$360 = 12z$
$30 = z$

$y = 3(30) = 90$

11. A $\dfrac{-2 \;\; 5}{-5 \;\; 2} = \dfrac{-2(5) - (-5)(2)}{-2(2) - (5)(-5)} = \dfrac{0}{21} = 0$

12. A $\dfrac{-1\mid -1}{-1\mid 2} = \dfrac{1+2}{-2-1} = \dfrac{3}{-3} = -1$

$\dfrac{\dfrac{-1\mid -1}{-1\mid 2}\mid -1}{-1\mid 2} = \dfrac{-1\mid -1}{-1\mid 2} = -1$

13. C $\left(\dfrac{3-2}{2}, \dfrac{-5+6}{2}\right) = \left(\dfrac{1}{2}, \dfrac{1}{2}\right)$

14. C A $155 + 2(67) + 3(70) = 499$
B $155 + 3(67) + 2(70) = 496$
C $155 + 4(67) + 70 = 493$
D $155 + 3(67) + 3(70) = 566$
E $155 + 4(67) + 2(70) = 563$

15. C

O	O	X
X	X	O
O	X	O

2 more O's are needed.

16. B $2a = 2$, so $1 < 2$

17. D The values of a and c vary.
$a + c = 22$

18. B $60° > 50°$
When $x = 50$, the shaded area of the rectangle is greater.

19. D $x^3 - 2y$ and $2y - x^3$ are additive inverses. The values of the expressions may be positive, negative, or zero.

20. C $\dfrac{1 \cdot 2 \cdot 3 \cdot 4}{6} = \dfrac{2 \cdot 3 \cdot 4}{6} =$

$\dfrac{2 \cdot 3 \cdot 2 \cdot 2}{6} = \dfrac{2 \cdot 2 \cdot 2 \cdot 3}{6}$

21. C $\dfrac{1}{4} = 0.25$

$\left(\dfrac{1}{4}\right)^3 = (0.25)^3$

22. D $a(-a) = -a^2 \qquad a + \dfrac{1}{a}$

If $a = -1$, $-a^2 > a + \dfrac{1}{a}$

If $a = 1$, $-a^2 < a + \dfrac{1}{a}$

23. B $X + 3 + 1 < 10$
$X + 4 < 10$

24. B $y < \dfrac{1}{2}y$

$x < y < \dfrac{1}{2}y < 0, x < \dfrac{1}{2}y$

25. A $180 - 130 = 50$
$180 - 120 = 60$
$50 + 60 + (180 - n) = 180$
$110 = n$

26. A $(x + 1)(x - 1) = x^2 - 1$
$x^2 > x^2 - 1$

27. C $\triangle PQR$ is equilateral
$m \angle PQR = 60, m \angle x = 60$
$\angle PQR$ and $\angle y$ are alternate interior angles and congruent. Therefore, $m \angle y = 60$.

28. C $P(R) = \dfrac{4}{12} = \dfrac{1}{3}$

$P(\sim(R \vee B)) = P(W) = \dfrac{4}{12} = \dfrac{1}{3}$

29. B $0 < x < 1, x^2 < 1$
$y < -1, y^2 > 1$
$y^2 > x^2$

30. A $x^5 > 0$
$y^5 < 0$
$x^5 > y^5$

31. D $(a \circ b)^2 = (a^2 - b^2)^2$
$\qquad = a^4 - 2a^2b^2 + b^4$
$a^2 \circ b^2 = (a^2)^2 - (b^2)^2 = a^4 - b^4$
If $a = 1$ and $b = 2$,
$(a \circ b)^2 > a^2 \circ b^2$
If $a = 5$ and $b = 1$,
$a^2 \circ b^2 > (a \circ b)^2$

32. A $p = \dfrac{3}{4}p + 0.75$

$\dfrac{1}{4}p = 0.75$

$p = 0.75(4)$
$p = \$3.00$

33. D There is a total of 9 parts, $3 + 4 + 2$.

$\dfrac{4}{9} = \dfrac{32}{x}$

$4x = 288$
$x = 72$

34. B $42xy = 6x \cdot 7y = 5 \cdot 6 = 30$

35. B $\dfrac{1}{2}y$ is a positive value, so $\left(-6, \dfrac{1}{2}y\right)$ must be in the second quadrant.

36. A $2.45 = r(35.00)$
$0.07 = r$
$7\% = r$

37. C Area of the triangle $= 30 = \dfrac{1}{2} \cdot b \cdot 15$

$30 = \dfrac{15}{2}b$

$4 = b$

38. C $1 - \dfrac{1}{4} = \dfrac{3}{4}$

$\dfrac{2}{3} \cdot \dfrac{3}{4} = \dfrac{6}{12} = \dfrac{1}{2}$

39. D $(x - y)^2 + 2xy =$
$x^2 - 2xy + y^2 + 2xy =$
$x^2 + y^2$

40. E $32 - 24 = 8 = BF$
$CB^2 + 8^2 = 10^2$
$\qquad CB^2 = 36$
$\qquad CB = 6$

Area $= 6(24) = 144$

41. B A $8, 10$ yes
B $9, 11$ no
C $12, 14$ yes
D $16, 18$ yes
E $49, 51$ yes

42. B $\dfrac{\dfrac{2}{5} + \dfrac{3}{7}}{\dfrac{6}{11}} = \dfrac{11}{6}\left(\dfrac{2}{5} + \dfrac{3}{7}\right)$

Take half of the value. The effect is doubling the 6.

$\dfrac{1}{2} \cdot \dfrac{11}{6}\left(\dfrac{2}{5} + \dfrac{3}{7}\right) = \dfrac{11}{12}\left(\dfrac{2}{5} + \dfrac{3}{7}\right)$

43. B 7 ligs $= 4$ wids $= 12$ gads
7 ligs $= 12$ gads, 1 wid $= 3$ gads

$\dfrac{7}{12}$ lig $= 1$ gad

3 wids $+ 2$ gads $= 9$ gads $+ 2$ gads $= 11$ gads
The least whole number of ligs greater than 11 gads:

11 gads $= 11 \cdot \dfrac{7}{12}$ lig $= \dfrac{77}{12}$ ligs $= 6\dfrac{5}{12}$ ligs

At least 7 ligs are needed.

44. D (I) $\frac{1}{3} + \frac{1}{3} + \frac{1}{3} = 1$

(II) $2 + \frac{1}{2} + \frac{1}{2} = 3$

(III) No

45. E $e > c > a$

$e > c > b$

$e > d$

46. E $12 \text{ ft} \times 12 \text{ ft} = 144 \text{ ft}^2$

$6 \text{ in.} \times 6 \text{ in.} = 36 \text{ in.}^2$

$1 \text{ ft}^2 = 144 \text{ in.}^2$

$36 \text{ in.}^2 = 36 \div 144 = \frac{1}{4} \text{ ft}^2$

$144 \div \frac{1}{4} = 144 \cdot 4 = 576$

47. D $1 \times 24 \quad P = 50$

$2 \times 12 \quad P = 28$

$3 \times 8 \quad P = 22$

$4 \times 6 \quad P = 20$

48. A Extend the sequence, . . . 39, 63, 102, . . .

Every third term is even. 18 is a multiple of 3; the 18th term is even.

49. C $d = rt$

$d = 50t$

$\frac{d}{50} = t$

50. B A = average

s = sum

$A = \frac{s}{n} = 0.1s$

$\frac{s}{n} = \frac{s}{10}$; if $s \ne 0$, then $n = 10$

EXAM 3

1. C $7 - x = x - 13$

$20 = 2x$

$10 = x$

2. D Areas C and D are common to I and III, but only D is not part of II.

3. B $\frac{c}{22}$

4. D $6 = 2 \cdot 3$

$15 = 3 \cdot 5$

$14 = 2 \cdot 7$

$\text{LCM} = 2 \cdot 3 \cdot 5 \cdot 7 = 210$

5. B $90 + 62 + x = 180$

$x = 28$

6. C $100 + 12(125) = 1600$

$1600 - 1300 = 300$

7. D $-(2 - 4)(-3) = -(-3)(2 - 4) =$

$3(2 - 4) = (2 - 4)(3)$

8. A $\left(r + \frac{1}{4}\right) + \left(r - \frac{1}{4}\right) = 7$

$2r = 7$

$r = \frac{7}{2}$

9. A $48 = \frac{5}{6}x$

$\frac{6}{5} \cdot 48 = x$

$\frac{288}{5} = x$

$57\frac{3}{5} = x$

10. A $x + y + x = 180$

$2x + y = 180$

$2x + 2x = 180$

$4x = 180$

$x = 45$

11. C $3 * 7 = 2(7) - 3 = 14 - 3 = 11$

12. B $-1 * 1 = 2(1) - (-1) = 2 + 1 = 3$

13. B $\left(\frac{-6 + -2}{2}, \frac{2 + -4}{2}\right) = (-4, -1)$

14. B $(45)3 = \$135$

$3(20) + 0.12(150) = \$78$

15. B

B	A	B
A	A	B
B	B	A

2 more A's are needed.

16. A Since $xy = 1$, $z = 0$.

$1 > 0$

17. D $x + y = 3 + y$

$x = 3$, y can be any real number.

18. C $m \angle B = 45$; $\triangle ABC$ is isosceles

19. D If $a = 0$, $a = -a$

If $a = 1$, $a > -a$

If $a = -1$, $-a > a$

20. C $\frac{2 \cdot 3 \cdot 4 \cdot 6}{7} = \frac{2 \cdot 3 \cdot 2 \cdot 2 \cdot 3}{7} =$

$\frac{2 \cdot 2 \cdot 2 \cdot 3 \cdot 3}{7}$

21. B $0.125 = \frac{1}{8}$

$\left(\frac{1}{8}\right)^3 < \left(\frac{1}{8}\right)^2$

$\frac{1}{512} < \frac{1}{64}$

22. C $(-a)(-b) = ab$

23. A $X + 6 + 1 \ge 10$

$X + 6 \ge 9$

$X + 6 > 8$

24. A $x < y$

$-x > -y$

25. B $180 - 110 = 70$

$180 - 80 = 100$

$70 + 100 + (180 - n) = 180$

$170 = n$

26. D If $x = 0$, $1 = x^2 + 1$

If $x \ne 0$, $x^2 > 0$ and $x^2 + 1 > 1$

27. C Corresponding angles are congruent.

28. C $P(R) = \frac{7}{10}$

$P(\sim B) = P(R) = \frac{7}{10}$

29. B $a < 0$, $a^3 < 0$

$b > 0$, $b^3 > 0$

30. A $b > 1 \rightarrow -b < -1$

$-1 < a < 0$

$-b < -1 < a$

$-b < a$

31. A $(a * b)^2 = (a^2 + b^4)^2 = a^4 + 2a^2b^4 + b^8$

$a^2 * b^2 = (a^2)^2 + (b^2)^4 = a^4 + b^8$

Since $2a^2b^4 > 0$,

$(a * b)^2 > a^2 * b^2$.

32. C $p = \frac{7}{10}p + 0.90$

$\frac{3}{10}p = 0.90$

$p = 0.90 \cdot \frac{10}{3}$

$p = \$3.00$

33. A There is a total of 9 parts, $4 + 3 + 2$.

$\frac{4}{9} = \frac{2300}{T}$

$4T = 20{,}700$

$T = 5175$

34. B $8xy = 2x \cdot 4y = 17 \cdot 11 = 187$

35. D Since $-x < 0$, $(x, -2)$ must be in the fourth quadrant.

36. C $X + Y = 15 + 25 = 40$

$2.80 = r(40)$

$0.07 = r$

$7\% = r$

37. C Area of the square $= 8 \cdot 8 = 64$

Area of the triangle $= 64 = \frac{1}{2} \cdot 16 \cdot h$

$64 = \frac{16}{2}h$

$8 = h$

38. E $\frac{1}{2}\left(\frac{2}{3}\right) = \frac{1}{3}$

39. B $(a - b)^2 + 4ab =$

$a^2 - 2ab + b^2 + 4ab =$

$a^2 + 2ab + b^2 =$

$(a + b)^2$

40. B $3^2 + AC^2 = 5^2$

$AC^2 = 16$

$AC = 4$

Area of $\triangle ABC = \frac{1}{2} \cdot 4 \cdot 6 = 12$

41. E $51 = 3 \cdot 17$

$57 = 3 \cdot 19$

$63 = 3 \cdot 21$

None of these is prime.

42. D $\dfrac{\frac{1}{2} + \frac{4}{3}}{\frac{5}{7}} = \frac{7}{5}\left(\frac{1}{2} + \frac{4}{3}\right)$

Triple the value. The effect is tripling the 7.

$3 \cdot \frac{7}{5}\left(\frac{1}{2} + \frac{4}{3}\right) = \frac{21}{5}\left(\frac{1}{2} + \frac{4}{3}\right)$

43. A $a = 2b$

$3b = 5c, b = \frac{5}{3}c$

Substitute for b in $a = 2b$.

$a = 2\left(\frac{5}{3}c\right)$

$a = \frac{10}{3}c$

$3a = 10c$

44. D (I) $\frac{2}{3} \cdot \frac{3}{2} = 1$

(II) $\frac{1}{3} \cdot 3 = 1$

(III) No

45. E $e > d > b > a$

$e > d > c$

46. A $6m \times 7m = 600 \text{ cm} \times 700 \text{ cm}$

$= 420{,}000 \text{ cm}^2$

$5 \text{ cm} \times 5 \text{ cm} = 25 \text{ cm}^2$

$420{,}000 \div 25 = 16{,}800$

47. D $1 \times 32, \quad P = 66$

$2 \times 16, \quad P = 36$

$4 \times 8, \quad\ \ P = 24$

48. C For each term a_n, $a_n = n^2 + 1$.

$a_{10} = 10^2 + 1 = 101$

49. C $d = rt$

$m = r3$

$\frac{m}{3} = r$

50. C $A = $ average

$s = $ sum

$A = \frac{s}{n} = 0.04s = \frac{4}{100}s = \frac{s}{25}$

$\frac{s}{n} = \frac{s}{25}$

If $s \neq 0$, then $n = 25$.

EXAM 4

1. C For m to be an integral multiple of 8, $\frac{m}{8}$ must be an integer.

If $m = 4$, $\frac{4}{8}$ is not an integer.

2. B A Venn diagram would show 10 in the intersection of set A and set B.

$50 + 30 - 10 = 70$

3. D $2(40) - 29 = 80 - 29 = 51$

4. D Division by 0 is undefined.

5. C $m \angle ACB = 28°$ (congruent to $\angle DCE$)

$90 + 28 + x = 180$

$x = 62$

6. B $7 \times 24 = 168$

7. D $(x + y) - (x - y) =$

$x + y - x + y = 2y$

8. C $2x - 3 = 6$

$2x = 9$

$x = \frac{9}{2}$

9. B $6x = 360$

$x = 60$

10. B 50 people is 5 times as many as 10 people.

$5 \cdot \frac{2}{3} = \frac{10}{3} = 3\frac{1}{3}$

11. A $\dfrac{3 \mid 2}{-3 \mid 2} = \dfrac{6 - (-6)}{-9 - 4} = -\dfrac{12}{13}$

12. A $\dfrac{1 \mid 1}{1 \mid 0} = \dfrac{1 - 0}{1 - 0} = 1$

$\dfrac{\frac{1 \mid 1}{1 \mid 0} \mid 1}{1 \mid 0} = \dfrac{1 \mid 1}{1 \mid 0} = 1$

13. D $\left(\dfrac{1 + 1}{2}, \dfrac{2 + 5}{2}\right) = \left(1, \dfrac{7}{2}\right)$

14. C A. $2(7.50) + 5.25 = 20.25$

B. $7.50 + 9.50 + 5.25 = 22.25$

C. $9.50 + 5.25 = 14.75$

D. $7.50 + 9.50 = 17$

E. $7.50 + 2(5.25) = 18$

15. D After 12 moves they were back to A.

13	14	15
A	B	C

After 15 moves it is D's move.

16. C $AB = 1$

$B = \frac{1}{A}$

17. A $2^4 = 16$, so $2^4 > 8$

18. C $C = \pi d$

$C = \pi 4$

length $AB = \frac{1}{4}C = \frac{1}{4}\pi 4 = \pi$

19. C $16 = 9 + x + 7 - y$

$16 = 16 + x - y$

$0 = x - y$

$x = y$

20. B $(x - y)(x + y) = x^2 - y^2$

$x^2 - y^2 < x^2$ since $y^2 > 0$

21. B $a + b + c = 180$

22. B $a\left(-\frac{1}{a}\right) = -1$

$a + -a = 0$

23. B Using the check for subtraction,

$Y + 5 + 1 < 10$

$Y + 6 < 10$

24. C 2 days begin with "T" and 2 days begin with "S."

$P(T) = \frac{2}{7}$ $P(S) = \frac{2}{7}$

25. A $m \angle y = m \angle z$ (corresponding angles)

$x = 180 - z$

$x + y = (180 - z) + z = 180$

26. A $x = 60(5)$

$\frac{x}{5} = \frac{60(5)}{5} = 60$

27. B $y + 2(90 - x) = 180$

$y + 180 - 2x = 180$

$y = 2x$

$x = 30, y = 60$

$3x = 90, 2y = 120$

28. B Square both expressions and compare.

$(\sqrt{a + b})^2 = a + b$

$(\sqrt{a} + \sqrt{b})^2 = a + 2\sqrt{a} \cdot \sqrt{b} + b$

$a + b < a + 2\sqrt{a} \cdot \sqrt{b} + b$

29. C $\triangle ABC$ is isosceles, so $AB = AC$.

$AB^2 + AB^2 = BC^2$

$2(AB)^2 = BC^2$

$AB\sqrt{2} = BC$

30. A $-3x < 6$

$x > -2$

31. D If $a = 2$, then $a > \frac{1}{a}$.

If $a = \frac{1}{2}$, then $\frac{1}{a} > a$.

32. A $10^{-2} = \frac{1}{100}, \frac{1}{100} < \frac{1}{10}$

33. C $y = \frac{k}{x}$

$9 = \frac{k}{3}$

$27 = k$

34. D $\frac{16}{25} = \frac{g}{r}$

35. C Quadrant III contains all points that have a negative value for both the x and the y coordinate.

36. D $0.70 = x(14)$

$0.05 = x$

$5\% = x$

37. D $A = s^2 = 49, s = 7$

$P = 4s = 4(7) = 28$

38. E $\frac{4}{5}\left(\frac{1}{2}\right) = \frac{2}{5}$

39. A $(a + b)^2 + (a - b)^2 =$

$(a^2 + 2ab + b^2) + (a^2 - 2ab + b^2) =$

$2a^2 + 2b^2 = 2(a^2 + b^2)$

40. D $AB^2 = 10^2 - 8^2 = 36$

$AB = 6$

Area $= \frac{1}{2}(6)(8) = 24$

41. C Since 1 has only one factor, it is not composite.

42. D $\dfrac{\frac{2}{3} + \frac{4}{5}}{\frac{6}{7}} = \frac{7}{6}\left(\frac{2}{3} + \frac{4}{5}\right)$

Find $\frac{1}{2}$ of the value. The effect is doubling the 6.

$\frac{1}{2} \cdot \frac{7}{6}\left(\frac{2}{3} + \frac{4}{5}\right) =$

$\frac{7}{12}\left(\frac{2}{3} + \frac{4}{5}\right)$

43. C $5n = q$ and $4q = d$

$4q = 4(5n) = 20n$

$20n = d$

$n = \frac{d}{20}$

44. A I. True; all positive factors yield a positive product.

II. False; 5 negative factors would result in a negative product.

III. False; there would have to be 0, 2, or 4 positive factors in the product. The remaining 5, 3, or 1 factors would be negative, resulting in a negative product.

45. B $b > a > c$

$b > a > d$

46. D Rate of the second hand:

$\frac{1 \text{ rotation}}{1 \text{ minute}}$

Rate of minute hand:

$\frac{1 \text{ rotation}}{60 \text{ minutes}}$

The rate of the second hand, 1 rotation/min, is 60 times the rate of the minute hand, 1 rotation/60 min.

47. C $1 \times 18, \quad P = 38$

$2 \times 9, \quad P = 22$

$3 \times 6, \quad P = 18$

48. D Every fourth term and its predecessor are even.

18, 54, 113, and 966 are not multiples of 4 or one less than a multiple of 4.

484 is a multiple of 4.

49. A Rate of discount $\times$ original price = amount of discount

$\frac{r}{100} \cdot a = b$

$r = \frac{b}{a} \cdot 100$

50. B $190 \times 22 = 4180$

Strategy Problem Bank Answers

STRATEGY PROBLEM BANK 1

1. Suggested strategy: Draw a diagram to show the movement of the bug. Answer: On the 11th day, the bug will reach the top of the jar.
2. Suggested strategy: Draw a diagram to show the positions of the runners. Answer: The order in which they finished was Otis, Scott, Carlos, Tom, Pat, Daniel.
3. Suggested strategy: Guess the number of dimes and nickels. Check. Revise your guess. Answer: Lian has 9 dimes (and 7 nickels).

STRATEGY PROBLEM BANK 2

1. Suggested strategy: Guess the number each student has to start with. Answer: Each student started with 9 posters.
2. Suggested strategy: Guess the number of dogs and parakeets. Check and revise your guess. Answer: The pet shop has 9 parakeets (and 6 dogs).
3. Suggested strategy: Draw a diagram to show the dimensions of the box. Answer: The volume is 120 cm³.

STRATEGY PROBLEM BANK 3

1. Suggested strategy: Make an organized list of all the combinations of 2 different pets. Answer: Ted has 10 possible choices.
2. Suggested strategy: Make an organized list of pairs of factors of 110. Answer: The possible dimensions are 1 cm × 110 cm, 2 cm × 55 cm, 5 cm × 22 cm, 11 cm × 10 cm. The rectangle with dimensions 1 cm × 110 cm has the greatest perimeter.
3. Suggested strategy: Guess the minutes. Check and revise your guess. Answer: Lydia can talk for 10 minutes (10.2 min would cost another $0.25).

STRATEGY PROBLEM BANK 4

1. Suggested strategy: Record the information in a table and make conclusions. Answer: Mr. Green's house is brown.
2. Suggested strategy: Draw a diagram of the trail and markers. Answer: She used 11 trail markers.
3. Suggested strategy: Use logical reasoning to interpret the data and make conclusions. Answer: 24 students belong only to the Science Club.

STRATEGY PROBLEM BANK 5

1. Suggested strategy: Make a table and look for a pattern. Answer: Ms. Guzman would have assigned 385 problems on the tenth day if she had continued the pattern.
2. Suggested strategy: Make a table and look for a pattern. How many handshakes for 2 people? for 3 people? Answer: There would be 105 handshakes.
3. Suggested strategy: Make a table and look for a pattern. Answer: It took 8 hours for the joke to spread to everyone in Jollyville.

STRATEGY PROBLEM BANK 6

1. Suggested strategy: Make an organized list of the choices. Answer: There are 20 possible sets to choose from.
2. Suggested strategy: Make a table showing the deposits. Answer: Inés will have put $693 into her account after 7 weeks.
3. Suggested strategy: Guess how many votes the winner received. Check and revise your guess. Answer: The winner received 24 votes.

STRATEGY PROBLEM BANK 7

1. Suggested strategy: Simplify the problem. How many color combinations for 2 colors? for 3 colors? for 4 colors? Then make a table and find a pattern. Answer: There are 153 different color combinations possible.

2. Suggested strategy: Simplify the problem(s). What is the sum of the first 2 numbers? 3 numbers? Make a table and look for a pattern. Answer: The sum of the first 100 nonzero even numbers is 10,100 (100 · 101). The sum of the first 100 odd numbers is 10,000 (100²).
3. Suggested strategy: Make a table of powers of 2 and look for a pattern. Answer: The ones digit is 2.

STRATEGY PROBLEM BANK 8

1. Suggested strategy: Make an organized list of combinations of pencils. Answer: There are 12 ways in which Leon can spend exactly $0.45 on pencils.
2. Suggested strategy: Guess, check, and revise. Answer: There are 6 men's dorm rooms (and 8 women's dorm rooms).
3. Suggested strategy: Make an organized list of page numbers. Answer: The report has 25 pages.

STRATEGY PROBLEM BANK 9

1. Suggested strategy: Guess the number of pies he ate the first day. Check and revise. Answer: The pie eating champion ate 10 pies the first day.
2. Suggested strategy: Draw a diagram that shows her progress. Answer: It would take Dana 7 hours to make the 6-mile trip.
3. Suggested strategy: Draw a diagram (Venn diagram, see page 376) depicting gidgets, widgets, and hidgets. Use logical reasoning to make conclusions. Answer: 10 widgets are not gidgets.

STRATEGY PROBLEM BANK 10

1. Suggested strategy: Work backward. Answer: Colleen started with $100.
2. Suggested strategy: Work backward. Answer: There are 95 coins in the bag.
3. Suggested strategy: Work backward. Answer: The men gathered 27 coconuts.

STRATEGY PROBLEM BANK 11

1. Suggested strategy: Draw a diagram of the large cube showing the cuts. Answer: Of the 27 small cubes, 8 are painted on three sides, 12 are painted on two sides, 6 are painted on one side, and 1 is painted on zero sides.
2. Suggested strategy: Write an equation. Answer: The batting glove costs $4 and the fielding glove costs $40.
3. Suggested strategy: Use logical reasoning. Answer: Jane plays water polo, Dan plays tennis, Kiri plays basketball, and Lon plays football.

STRATEGY PROBLEM BANK 12

1. Suggested strategy: Write an equation. Then guess, check, and revise your guess. Answer: Toshi needs at least a total of 398 points, or 18 more points, to get a grade of 80%.
2. Suggested strategy: Guess the lengths of the sides. Then check. Answer: The shortest side can be 1, 2, 3, or 4 units long. The longest side can be 6, 7, 8, or 9 units long.
3. Suggested strategy: Draw a diagram and use logical reasoning. Answer: Fill the 9-cup container and use the 4-cup container to remove 8 cups. Pour the 1 cup left in the 9-cup container into the empty 4-cup container. Fill the 9-cup container, and pour water from it to finish filling the 4-cup container, which will hold 3 more cups. This will leave 6 cups of water in the 9-cup container.

STRATEGY PROBLEM BANK 13

1. Suggested strategy: Simplify the problem. How many tournament games are needed for 2 teams? 3 teams? Make a table and find a pattern. Answer: 13 games are needed to determine the champion.

2. Suggested strategy: Make an organized list and/or draw a diagram. Answer: 28 choices of checkbook covers are available.
3. Suggested strategy: Draw a diagram. Answer: The water will reach the top of the tank on the 9th day.

STRATEGY PROBLEM BANK 14

1. Suggested strategy: Write an equation. Answer: Consultant 1 made $7520, Consultant 2 made $6620, and Consultant 3 made $6820.
2. Suggested strategy: Make a table and use logical reasoning to make conclusions. Answer: Mr. Bettis is Kea's father.

3. Suggested strategy: Work backward. Answer: Luis deposited $751.32 three years ago.

STRATEGY PROBLEM BANK 15

1. Suggested strategy: Write an equation. Answer: Melissa needs at least 89 points on the final exam to average 85 for the course.
2. Suggested strategy: Work backward. Answer: 176 calves must be born for the farmer to have 100 male calves at the end of the first year.
3. Suggested strategy: Make a table and look for a pattern. Answer: The sum is 3025.

Problem Bank Answers

PROBLEM BANK 1

1. $a - 5$ 2. $\frac{1}{3}p$ or $\frac{p}{3}$ 3. $c + 80$ 4. $\frac{t}{6}$ or $\frac{1}{6}t$

5. $a - 23$ 6. $12 - x$ or $\frac{24 - 2x}{2}$ 7. $s - 5$ 8. $j + 8$

9. $\frac{72}{y}$ 10. $2m + 3$

PROBLEM BANK 2

1. $1031.36 2. $-11°F$ 3. 9-yd gain 4. $6.56
5. 14.75 m 6. +$20,860

PROBLEM BANK 3

1. $-$234.11 2. 7°C 3. 401 students 4. 32 ft
5. 21 floors 6. $-14°C$ 7. 19 m 8. $43 9. $-$4.20

PROBLEM BANK 4

1. Let p be the number of points scored in the first game.
   $p + 4 = 16$ or $16 - 4 = p$
2. Let f be the number of freshmen.
   $f + 215 = 434$ or $434 - 215 = f$
3. Let p be the number of people who bought tickets.
   $p \cdot 2.25 = 276.75$ or $p = 276.75 \div 2.25$
4. Let h be the hourly rate of pay.
   $h \cdot 7 = 154$ or $h = 154 \div 7$
5. Let c be the cost of one ounce.
   $c \cdot 6 = 2.55$ or $c = 2.55 \div 6$
6. Let j be the length of the second best jump.
   $j + 3.1 = 5.4$ or $j = 5.4 - 3.1$
7. Let b be the boiling point of ethyl alcohol.
   $b + 21.7 = 100$ or $b = 100 - 21.7$
8. Let h be the height of the Statue of Liberty.
   $\frac{1}{5}h = 18.5$ or $h = 5 \cdot 18.5$
9. Let s be the score of the other team.
   $s + 105 = 180$ or $s = 180 - 105$
10. Let w be the width of the rectangle.
    $w \cdot 9 = 72$ or $w = 72 \div 9$

PROBLEM BANK 5

1. 29 2. 24 years old 3. $8220 4. $0.54
5. 5605 calendars 6. $143.48 7. 525 compact discs
8. $1688.53 9. 12°C

PROBLEM BANK 6

1. -12 2. 36 3. $0.19 4. $1250 5. $0.39
6. 387 people 7. 235 tapes 8. $1,018,350, $339,450
9. 700 students 10. $70

PROBLEM BANK 7

1. $\frac{V}{\pi h}$ 2. $\frac{2d}{t^2}$ 3. $\frac{2s - gt^2}{2t}$ or $\frac{s - \frac{1}{2}gt^2}{t}$ 4. $\frac{2(s - vt)}{t^2}$

5. $\frac{a}{(1 + r)^t}$ 6. $\frac{c}{2r}$ 7. $\frac{P - 2l}{2}$ 8. $\frac{F - 32}{1.8}$

9. $\frac{s - 4.9t^2}{t}$ 10. $\frac{y - y_1}{x - x_1}$

PROBLEM BANK 8

1. 366 students 2. 65 ducks 3. 1560 red marbles
4. 15.5 h 5. 399.5 mi 6. 95 km 7. 24,128 voters
8. 462 carp 9. 28 points

PROBLEM BANK 9

1. 75% 2. 115% 3. $2730 4. $24.23, $370.43

PROBLEM BANK 10

5. 45.65 cm³, 504.35 cm³ 6. $5.60, $145.60 7. $150
8. 4590 bears, 4682 bears

1. 12 years 2. 29, 30, 31 3. 26, 28, 30 4. $55
5. 5 in., 8 in., 10 in. 6. $72 7. $5500
8. 1176 students 9. 19 oz 10. 44 games

PROBLEM BANK 11

1. 22, 24, 26 2. 12, 27 3. 8, 19 4. greater than 3 cm
5. 15 boxes or more 6. $680 or more 7. $43
8. greater than 15 m 9. greater than 8 cm

PROBLEM BANK 12

1. 6, 8 2. 4 in., 8 in. 3. $-12, -10; 10, 12$ 4. -1
5. 3 or 2 6. 5 seconds 7. 12 m, 52 m² 8. 0 or 3
9. 10 mm, 5 mm

PROBLEM BANK 13

1. a. $c = 0.2w + 5.78$ b. $12.18
2. a. $K = C + 273.15$ b. 303.15 K
3. a. $F = 1.8K - 459.67$ b. 212°F
4. a. $w = \frac{4}{5}h - 70$ b. 62 kg
5. a. $f = 0.6d + 0.75$ b. $19.95
6. a. $b = -\frac{4}{5}a + 176$ b. 164

PROBLEM BANK 14

1. 16, 23 2. 6, 18 3. 29, 12 4. 20, 42 5. 18, 27
6. 8, 6 7. $-7, 3$ 8. $17, -6$ 9. $5\frac{4}{9}, 10\frac{4}{9}$
10. 20 cm, 9 cm

PROBLEM BANK 15

1. $-189, 252$ 2. 50, 15 3. 64, 33 4. 4.72, 18.88
5. $14, -6$ 6. $\frac{1}{2}, \frac{3}{4}$ 7. 21°, 69° 8. 80°, 100°
9. 113 cm, 53 cm 10. $7, -8$

PROBLEM BANK 16

1. Chim 34, Jared 8 2. 75 adult, 45 student
3. 80 ticks, 100 mosquitoes 4. 19 rectangular, 6 hexagonal
5. 18 girls, 4 boys 6. Elisa, 13, Ira 34
7. Karen, $34, Gil, $36 8. sport, $53.18, dress, $37.30
9. 8 with rock band pictures, 22 with names

PROBLEM BANK 17

1. 3 h, no 2. 6 h after Fred left, 4 h after Celia left
3. 3 a.m. 4. 20 min or $\frac{1}{3}$h
5. 1.5 mi/h current, 3 mi/h rowing 6. 60 mi/h
7. 1.5 h after the express left, 3.5 h after the freight left

PROBLEM BANK 18

1. 18 dimes, 6 nickels 2. 97 3. 72 wheat, 353 oats
4. 15 quarters, 50 dimes 5. 43 6. $8.00
7. 13 muffins, 5 rolls 8. 11 dimes, 27 nickels

PROBLEM BANK 19

1. $4\frac{4}{5}$ h 2. $7\frac{1}{2}$ h 3. $\frac{21}{10}$ or $2\frac{1}{10}$ 4. $17\frac{1}{7}$ min
5. Dennis, 16 h; Juanita, 48 h 6. $4\frac{4}{9}$ h 7. $12, -12$
8. $20, -4$ 9. new press, 16 min; old press, 48 min

PROBLEM BANK 20

1. 30 mL of 30%, 70 mL of 70%   **2.** 37.5 L of 20%, 62.5 L of 60%

3. 145 gal   **4.** 112 L   **5.** $33\frac{1}{3}$ oz of 25%, $41\frac{2}{3}$ oz of 70%

6. 6 kg of pecans, 4 kg of almonds
7. $31,500 at 13.5%, $21,200 at 15%   **8.** 3.2 gal

9. $\frac{1}{6}$ gal or 0.17 gal

PROBLEM BANK 21

1. Yes, the ladder will reach about 28.7 ft, which is 3.3 ft from the top of the castle. They will be able to reach the top from the ladder and climb over.
2. Yes, the brace will need to be about 5.8 ft or about 5 ft 10 in.
3. Polson-Ronan road would cost $34,684.71 less   **4.** 8.5 cm
5. 9.9 in.

PROBLEM BANK 22

1. ≈101 m   **2.** ≈737 m   **3.** ≈4432 m   **4.** 45 ft
5. 320 ft   **6.** 64   **7.** 4   **8.** 81   **9.** 144.9 ft

PROBLEM BANK 23

1. $f(x) = 1.25x + 24$, $52.75   **2.** $f(x) = 6.75x + 35$, $1250

3. $f(x) = \frac{x}{4} + 50$, 54 cm   **4.** $f(x) = 0.12x + 15$, $43.80

5. $f(x) = 0.2x + 0.5$, $2.50
6. $f(x) = 12.75x + 9.98$, $35.48
7. $f(x) = 45x + 8.75$, $233.75

8. $f(x) = \frac{4.8x}{1000} + 5.15$, $12.35

9. $f(x) = 15(x - 1) + 30$ or $f(x) = 15x + 15$, $41.25

PROBLEM BANK 24

1. $3.52   **2.** 345 lb   **3.** 400 mi   **4.** $250.25
5. $0.30   **6.** 21 m   **7.** $64,800   **8.** $2.52

PROBLEM BANK 25

1. $12.25   **2.** 7 revolutions, 210 in.   **3.** 8 mm, 264 mm²
4. 67.5 min, 60,750 L   **5.** 3.9 h, 195 mi   **6.** 5 amperes
7. 20 minutes, 10,000 m or 10 km   **8.** 10 cm, 180 cm³

PROBLEM BANK 26

1. 1 cm   **2.** 5 m, 12 m   **3.** 17 cm, 10 cm   **4.** 8 km/h
5. 2 m and 4 m   **6.** 0.5 cm
7. Kathleen 50 mi/h, Stanley 60 mi/h
8. $w = 3$ in., $l = 4$ in., $d = 5$ in.   **9.** $h = 2$ mm, $b = 7$ mm

PROBLEM BANK 27

1. 6.2 m   **2.** 38.6 m   **3.** 174.1 m   **4.** 332.6 m
5. 6.4 ft, 11.1 ft   **6.** 217 m   **7.** 311.5 m   **8.** 0.7 km
9. 23.8 m   **10.** 1427.2 ft

College Entrance Exam Answers

EXAM 1

1. C	2. E	3. D	4. E	5. B	6. D	7. E
8. B	9. A	10. A	11. C	12. D	13. C	
14. E	15. C	16. A	17. D	18. A	19. D	
20. C	21. B	22. A	23. A	24. D	25. B	
26. D	27. B	28. C	29. A	30. B	31. A	
32. C	33. E	34. B	35. A	36. E	37. B	
38. A	39. B	40. E	41. E	42. E	43. C	
44. E	45. E	46. D	47. B	48. D	49. A	
50. C						

EXAM 2

1. C	2. D	3. A	4. D	5. D	6. D	7. E
8. B	9. B	10. B	11. A	12. A	13. C	
14. C	15. C	16. B	17. D	18. B	19. D	
20. C	21. C	22. D	23. B	24. D	25. A	
26. A	27. C	28. C	29. B	30. A	31. D	
32. A	33. D	34. B	35. B	36. A	37. C	
38. C	39. D	40. E	41. B	42. B	43. B	
44. D	45. E	46. E	47. D	48. A	49. C	
50. B						

EXAM 3

1. C	2. D	3. B	4. D	5. B	6. C	7. D
8. A	9. A	10. A	11. C	12. B	13. B	
14. B	15. B	16. A	17. D	18. C	19. D	
20. C	21. B	22. C	23. A	24. A	25. B	
26. D	27. C	28. C	29. B	30. A	31. A	
32. C	33. A	34. B	35. D	36. C	37. C	
38. E	39. B	40. B	41. E	42. D	43. A	
44. D	45. E	46. A	47. D	48. C	49. C	
50. C						

EXAM 4

1. C	2. B	3. D	4. D	5. C	6. B	7. D
8. C	9. B	10. B	11. A	12. A	13. D	
14. C	15. D	16. C	17. A	18. C	19. C	
20. B	21. B	22. B	23. B	24. C	25. A	
26. A	27. B	28. B	29. C	30. A	31. D	
32. A	33. C	34. D	35. C	36. D	37. D	
38. E	39. A	40. D	41. C	42. D	43. C	
44. A	45. B	46. C	47. C	48. D	49. A	
50. B						